Better Homes and Gardens

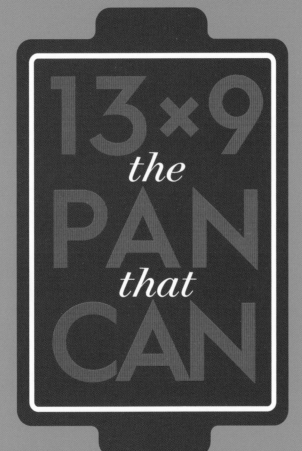

13×9 *the* PAN *that* CAN

150 Fabulous Recipes

HOUGHTON MIFFLIN HARCOURT
BOSTON · NEW YORK · 2017

BETTER HOMES AND GARDENS® 13×9 THE PAN THAT CAN

Editor: Jan Miller

Project Editor: Shelli McConnell, Purple Pear Publishing, Inc.

Contributing Editor: Ellen Boeke, Purple Pear Publishing, Inc.

Contributing Copy Editor and Proofreader: Peg Smith, Carrie Truesdell

Test Kitchen Director: Lynn Blanchard

Test Kitchen Product Supervisor: Colleen Weeden

Test Kitchen Home Economists: Sarah Brekke, Linda Brewer,
Carla Christian, Julie Hale, Sammy Mila

Contributing Photographers: Jason Donnelly, Jacob Fox, Andy Lyons

Contributing Stylists: Greg Luna, Dianna Nolin, Charlie Worthington

Administrative Assistants: Barb Allen, Marlene Todd

BETTER HOMES AND GARDENS®

Editor in Chief: Stephen Orr

Creative Director: Jennifer D. Madara

Editorial Director, Special Interest Publications: Jennifer Dorland Darling

Senior Art Director, Special Interest Publications: Stephanie Hunter

HOUGHTON MIFFLIN HARCOURT

Editorial Director: Cindy Kitchel

Executive Editor, Brands: Anne Ficklen

Editorial Associate: Molly Aronica

Managing Editor: Marina Padakis Lowry

Art Director: Tai Blanche

Production Director: Tom Hyland

WATERBURY PUBLICATIONS, INC.

Design Director: Ken Carlson

Associate Design Director: Doug Samuelson

Associate Editor: Tricia Bergman

Our seal assures you that every recipe in *Better Homes and Gardens® 13×9 The Pan That Can* has been tested in the Better Homes and Gardens® Test Kitchen. This means that each recipe is practical and reliable and meets our high standards of taste appeal. We guarantee your satisfaction with this book for as long as you own it.

Pictured on front cover:
Creamy Chicken Enchiladas, page 82; Zoodle Pizza Casserole, page 92; Pistachio-Cranberry Baklava, page 241; Fudgy Brownies, page 232; Citrus-Honey Sweet Rolls, page 60; Gingered Cherry Cobbler, page 256; Cheesy Potato Bake with Eggs, page 44

Pictured on back cover:
Quinoa Caprese Casserole, page 100; Za'atar Rice-Stuffed Peppers, page 139; Greek Chicken and Pita Casserole, page 114; Chocolate Chip Cookie Cake, page 268

CONTENTS

KNOW YOUR PAN

A 13×9-inch baking pan (made of metal) is equivalent to a 3-quart rectangular baking dish (usually made of glass or stoneware). They can be used interchangeably in recipes, though their dimensions may vary slightly depending on the manufacturer.

Because a 13×9-inch baking pan has a volume of 3 quarts, you can use it in any recipe that calls for a 3-quart casserole. A casserole is typically round or oval with a lid and is deeper than the 13×9-inch pan. Because of the pans shallow depth, food will cook faster and more evenly.

A 13×9-inch pan is almost twice the size of an 8-inch square pan. You can easily double recipes such as bars, brownies, and coffee cakes made in the smaller pan.

GLASS
Glass baking dishes are excellent for all-purpose baking. Glass is a nonreactive surface, which is necessary for citrusy dishes, egg casseroles, and tomato dishes. These acidic ingredients can discolor food and produce an off flavor if made in a pan with a reactive metal surface, such as aluminum. When baking in glass, never turn on the broiler or add cold ingredients to a hot dish. Glass dishes can shatter easily with sudden temperature changes.

METAL
Metal pans are most often used for baking cakes, bars, and brownies. They're usually made of steel, aluminized steel, or aluminum, and some have nonstick surfaces.

STONEWARE AND CAST IRON
Like glass, stoneware is a good nonreactive baking dish. But unlike glass, it can usually be put under a broiler. Check the manufacturer's directions to be sure. To avoid cracking, cool the dish completely before cleaning.

SERVING-SIZE MATH

Divide your pan to get the desired number of servings for baked foods that cut easily, such as bars, pan pies, or pizzas. Make the number of cuts described in the chart, being sure to space equally.

NUMBER OF CUTS		NUMBER OF SERVINGS
Lengthwise	Crosswise	
1	3	8
2	2	9
2	3	12
3	3	16
3	4	20
3	5	24
4	4	25
4	5	30
3	7	32
3	8	36
4	7	40
5	7	48
5	9	60
7	7	64

PAN POINTERS

FOIL YOUR PAN

Line a pan with foil for easy removal of bars, cakes, and brownies and for quick cleanup. To line a pan, turn it upside down and shape the foil over the outside, extending the foil about 1 inch past pan edges. Lift the foil off the pan, turn the pan over, and place the shaped foil inside the pan. Grease the foil if the recipe specifies. Use the foil to lift the baked food out of the pan.

VOLUME CHECK

If you are not sure of a pan's capacity, fill it with water, 1 quart at a time.

SLICK PREP

When a recipe calls for greasing a pan or dish, dip a piece of waxed paper or paper towel in shortening and wipe the pan with a light coating. Or use a light coating of nonstick cooking spray.

MAKE-IT-MINE
STUFFED
MUSHROOMS
Recipe on page 23

START THE PARTY

CHEESY ARTICHOKE DIP

PREP 30 minutes **RISE** 1 hour **BAKE** 30 minutes at 375°F **STAND** 10 minutes

1 15- to 16-oz. pkg. frozen white dinner rolls, thawed (12 rolls)

1 8-oz. pkg. cream cheese, softened

1 8-oz. carton sour cream

¼ cup milk

1 8-oz. pkg. shredded Italian-blend cheeses

2 14-oz. cans artichoke hearts, drained and chopped

3 cups chopped fresh baby spinach

½ cup sliced green onions

2 cloves garlic, minced

1 Tbsp. butter, melted

1 Tbsp. grated Parmesan cheese

1. Divide each roll into two portions. Shape each portion into a small ball, pulling edges under to make a smooth top. Place rolls 2 to 3 inches apart on a floured sheet of parchment paper or waxed paper. Lightly cover and let rise 1 to 1½ hours or until nearly double in size.

2. Preheat oven to 375°F. In an extra-large bowl beat cream cheese with a mixer on medium to high 30 seconds. Add sour cream and milk; beat until combined. Beat in 1½ cups of the Italian-blend cheeses. Stir in artichokes, spinach, green onions, and garlic. Spread artichoke mixture into a 13×9-inch baking pan or 3-qt. rectangular baking dish. Sprinkle remaining Italian-blend cheeses over top.

3. Bake 15 minutes. Remove from oven. Arrange rolls on top of hot dip. Lightly brush roll tops with melted butter. Sprinkle rolls with Parmesan cheese.

4. Bake 15 to 20 minutes more or until rolls are golden and dip is hot. Let stand 10 minutes before serving.

NUMBER OF SERVINGS 24 (3 Tbsp. and 1 roll each)

PER SERVING *147 cal., 8 g fat (5 g sat. fat), 24 mg chol., 242 mg sodium, 13 g carb., 1 g fiber, 2 g sugars, 5 g pro.*

Prepare as directed through Step 2 except do not preheat oven. Cover surface of dip with plastic wrap and refrigerate up to 4 hours. Continue as directed, baking 20 minutes in Step 3.

Use reduced-fat versions of the cream cheese and sour cream to cut some fat without sacrificing flavor.

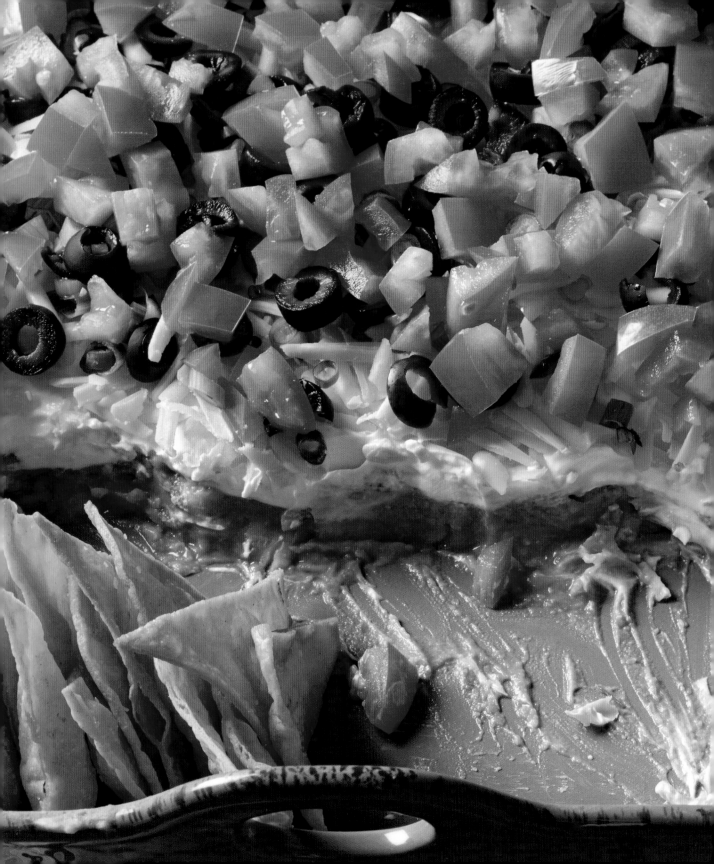

MEXICAN SEVEN-LAYER DIP

PREP 20 minutes **CHILL** 4 hours

- 2 16-oz. cans refried beans
- 1 cup bottled salsa
- 1 14-oz. pkg. refrigerated guacamole
- 1 16-oz. carton sour cream
- 2 cups shredded cheddar or taco cheese (8 oz.)
- ½ cup sliced green onions
- ½ cup sliced pitted ripe olives
- 2 cups chopped, seeded tomatoes
- 16 cups tortilla chips

1. In a bowl stir together refried beans and salsa; spread into a 3-qt. rectangular baking dish. Carefully layer guacamole and sour cream over bean mixture. Top with cheese, green onions, and olives. Cover and chill at least 4 hours.

2. Before serving, sprinkle with chopped tomatoes. Serve with tortilla chips.

NUMBER OF SERVINGS 32 (¼ cup dip and ½ cup chips each)

PER SERVING 179 cal., 11 g fat (4 g sat. fat), 15 mg chol., 340 mg sodium, 16 g carb., 3 g fiber, 1 g sugars, 5 g pro.

Prepare as directed through Step 1. Cover and refrigerate up to 24 hours before serving. Serve as directed.

There are some products that you would never know by taste that they are reduced-fat. If you are counting calories and watching fat, swap in fat-free refried beans, light sour cream, and reduced-fat cheese.

MAKE-IT-MINE NACHOS

PREP 15 minutes **BAKE** 20 minutes at 350°F

Make and serve this popular bar food in the same pan. Choose your chips, then use this formula to top them any way you like. Make sure the ingredients are evenly sprinkled over the chips so each bite has a little of everything. Serving a mixed crowd? Top half for those who like it hot and half for those who prefer mild.

5 cups bite-size tortilla chips (6 oz.)

Meat

1 15-oz. can Beans, rinsed and drained

1 cup chunky salsa

1½ cups shredded Cheese (6 oz.)

Toppings

1. Preheat oven to 350°F. Spread half the chips in an 13×9-inch pan. In a bowl combine Meat, Beans, and the 1 cup salsa. Spoon half the meat mixture over the chips. Sprinkle with half the Cheese.

2. Bake about 10 minutes or until cheese is melted. Top with remaining chips, meat mixture, and Cheese. Bake 10 minutes more or until cheese is melted. Top with desired Toppings.

NUMBER OF SERVINGS 8

MEAT

* 12 oz. ground beef, browned and drained
* 2 cups shredded cooked beef
* 2 cups chopped cooked chicken breast
* 2 cups shredded cooked pork

BEANS

* Black beans
* Pinto beans
* Small red beans
* White beans (Great Northern or cannellini)

CHEESE

* Cheddar cheese
* Co-Jack cheese
* Monterey Jack with jalapeños
* Mexican-style four-cheese blend

TOPPINGS

* Chili powder
* Chunky salsa
* Seeded and sliced fresh jalapeño chile peppers* or pickled jalapeño chile peppers
* Sliced green onions
* Sliced pitted ripe olives
* Snipped fresh cilantro
* Sour cream
* Guacamole

*TIP Chile peppers contain oils that can irritate your skin and eyes. Wear plastic or rubber gloves when working with them.

HAM BALLS IN BARBECUE SAUCE

PREP 20 minutes **BAKE** 25 minutes at 350°F

Grind the ham yourself for this recipe (pulse it in a food processor) or check at the meat counter of your supermarket. They can grind it for you, or they might have a ground ham loaf mixture that is equal parts ham and ground pork.

  2 eggs, lightly beaten

1½ cups soft bread crumbs

  ½ cup finely chopped onion

  2 Tbsp. milk

  ¼ tsp. black pepper

  2 tsp. dry mustard

 12 oz. ground cooked ham

 12 oz. ground pork or beef

  ¾ cup packed brown sugar

  ½ cup ketchup

  2 Tbsp. vinegar

1. Preheat oven to 350°F. Lightly grease a 3-qt. rectangular baking dish. In a large bowl combine the first five ingredients (through pepper); stir in 1 tsp. of the mustard. Add ground ham and pork; mix well. Shape mixture into 24 balls, using about 3 Tbsp. mixture for each. Arrange ham balls in the prepared baking dish.

2. For sauce, in a bowl stir together the remaining 1 tsp. mustard and remaining ingredients; pour over ham balls. Bake about 25 minutes or until done (160°F).

NUMBER OF SERVINGS 24 (1 ham ball each)

PER SERVING *92 cal., 3 g fat (1 g sat. fat), 34 mg chol., 204 mg sodium, 10 g carb., 0 g fiber, 8 g sugars, 6 g pro.*

CHICKEN AND EGGPLANT STUFFED SHELLS

PREP 30 minutes **BAKE** 18 minutes at 375°F

Olive oil nonstick cooking spray

12 dried jumbo shell macaroni

⅓ cup chopped onion

⅓ cup chopped red sweet pepper

1 Tbsp. olive oil

¾ cup chopped eggplant

2 cloves garlic, minced

¼ tsp. fennel seeds, crushed

½ cup chopped cooked chicken breast

½ cup crumbled feta cheese (2 oz.)

1 egg, lightly beaten

⅓ cup seasoned fine dry bread crumbs

⅓ cup fresh basil, thinly sliced

¾ cup marinara sauce, warmed

1. Preheat oven to 375°F. Line a 13×9-inch baking pan with foil; coat foil with cooking spray. Cook macaroni shells according to package directions; drain. Rinse with cold water; drain again. Invert shells on paper towels to dry.

2. Meanwhile, in a medium skillet cook onion and sweet pepper in hot olive oil over medium heat 3 minutes, stirring occasionally. Add eggplant, garlic, and fennel seeds. Cook 3 to 4 minutes more or until vegetables are tender, stirring occasionally. Remove from heat; stir in chicken and feta cheese.

3. Pour egg into a small bowl. Pour bread crumbs into another small bowl. Dip the outsides of each pasta shell in the egg, allowing excess to drip off. Dip coated shell in bread crumbs, turning to coat the whole outside with crumbs. Lightly coat outsides of shells with cooking spray. Place coated shells in the prepared pan, crumb sides down. Spoon chicken mixture evenly into shells.

4. Bake 18 to 20 minutes or until heated and bread crumbs are lightly browned. Transfer shells to a platter and sprinkle with basil. Serve with marinara sauce.

NUMBER OF SERVINGS 12 (1 filled shell and 1 Tbsp. sauce each)

PER SERVING 104 cal., 4 g fat (1 g sat. fat), 26 mg chol., 198 mg sodium, 12 g carb., 1 g fiber, 2 g sugars, 6 g pro.

BABY POTATOES ROASTED IN SALT

PREP 25 minutes **ROAST** 45 minutes at 425°F **COOL** 5 minutes

Don't be shocked by the amount of salt—it's not intended to be eaten. The salt provides a bed on which to bake and flavor the baby potatoes, and it adds a striking presentation.

¼ cup olive oil

4 cloves garlic, minced

3 Tbsp. snipped fresh
rosemary

30 small new potatoes and/or
fingerling potatoes (about
3 lb.)

1½ lb. kosher salt (3 cups)

¼ cup all-purpose flour

½ cup water

Freshly ground black
pepper

1. Preheat oven to 425°F. In a bowl combine 2 Tbsp. of the olive oil and the garlic. Brush mixture on the bottom and sides of a 3-qt. rectangular baking dish. Sprinkle rosemary over bottom of dish. Place potatoes in a single layer on top of rosemary.

2. In a large bowl combine salt and flour. Gradually stir in the water until combined. Spoon salt mixture evenly over potatoes, pressing firmly.

3. Roast 45 to 50 minutes or until potatoes are tender. Cool in pan on a wire rack 5 minutes. Using a thin metal spatula, loosen the salt crust from the side of the dish. Carefully invert potatoes and salt crust onto a large serving platter. Drizzle potatoes with the remaining 2 Tbsp. olive oil and sprinkle with pepper.

NUMBER OF SERVINGS 15 (2 potatoes each)

PER SERVING *105 cal., 4 g fat (1 g sat. fat), 0 mg chol., 1,163 mg sodium, 17 g carb., 2 g fiber, 1 g sugars, 2 g pro.*

BACON-FILLED MEDJOOL DATES

PREP 25 minutes **BAKE** 12 minutes at 375°F

- 6 slices bacon
- ½ cup whole almonds or pecan halves, toasted* and chopped
- ½ cup finely shredded Manchego or Parmesan cheese (2 oz.)
- 24 unpitted whole Medjool dates (about 1 lb.)
- 3 Tbsp. honey
- 1 tsp. snipped fresh thyme

1. Preheat oven to 375°F. In a large skillet cook bacon over medium heat until crisp. Transfer bacon to paper towels to drain; crumble bacon. In a bowl stir together the bacon, almonds, and cheese.

2. Make a slit down one side of each date and remove pit. Spoon about 1 Tbsp. of the bacon mixture into each date; press date to shape around filling (filling will still be visible). Arrange dates, filling sides up, in an ungreased 13×9-inch baking pan.

3. Bake 12 to 15 minutes or until heated through and cheese is lightly browned; cool slightly. Before serving, drizzle warm dates with honey and sprinkle with thyme.

NUMBER OF SERVINGS 24 (1 filled date each)

*TIP To toast nuts, seeds, or coconut, preheat oven to 350°F. Spread them in a shallow baking pan. Bake 5 to 10 minutes or until lightly browned, shaking pan once or twice.

PER SERVING *112 cal., 3 g fat (1 g sat. fat), 4 mg chol., 79 mg sodium, 21 g carb., 2 g fiber, 18 g sugars, 2 g pro.*

Prepare as directed through Step 2. Cover and refrigerate up to 2 days. Continue as directed, baking 15 to 18 minutes.

MAKE-IT-MINE STUFFED MUSHROOMS

Stuffed mushrooms are perfect party food. Make as many as you need—2 to 3 mushrooms per guest—and try a few different toppers for variety in flavor, texture, and color.

1½- to 2-inch button mushrooms

Nonstick cooking spray

Baking the Mushrooms Place cleaned and stemmed mushroom caps, stem sides down, in a 13×9-inch baking pan. Lightly coat with nonstick cooking spray. Bake in a 425°F oven 5 minutes. Drain, stem sides down, on paper towels; fill.

PICK THE FILLINGS

* **Beef and Blue** Thinly sliced roast beef, steamed asparagus tips, and crumbled blue cheese.

* **Ham and Sweet Potato** Chopped cooked ham, chopped cooked sweet potato, finely chopped green sweet pepper, and minced fresh garlic.

* **Egg Salad** Shredded fresh spinach, chopped hard-cooked egg, and quartered cherry tomato.

* **Bacon and Apple** Thinly sliced apple, shredded smoked cheddar cheese, and crumbled crisp-cooked bacon.

* **Cran-Turkey** Shredded smoked turkey, cranberry relish, and fresh sage leaves.

* **Cheesy Shrimp** Boursin cheese spread, mayonnaise, cooked medium shrimp, and fresh thyme leaves.

* **Chile Cream Cheese** Softened cream cheese, raspberry preserves, and sliced jalapeño chile pepper (tip, page 14).

* **Wasabi Chicken** Shredded cooked chicken, shredded carrot, sliced green onion, minced fresh ginger, and prepared wasabi paste.

* **Sausage Pizza** Cooked bulk Italian sausage, pizza sauce, shredded mozzarella cheese, and fresh parsley leaves.

* **Mediterranean** Prepared hummus, slivered oil-packed dried tomatoes, and sliced green and black olives.

PEACH SUNRISE COCKTAIL CUBES

PREP 15 minutes **CHILL** 3 hours

Who says jiggly treats are just for kids? Toss a few cubes in a cocktail glass, dress them up with a tiny umbrella, and let the party begin!

3 3-oz. pkg. orange-flavor gelatin

1½ cups boiling water

1½ cups cranberry juice

¾ cup vodka

6 Tbsp. peach schnapps

Nonstick cooking spray

1. In a bowl stir together gelatin and boiling water until completely dissolved. Add cranberry juice, vodka, and schnapps.

2. Coat a 3-qt. rectangular baking dish with cooking spray. Pour gelatin mixture into dish. Chill about 3 hours or until firm. Cut into 1-inch squares. Serve in cocktail glasses.

NUMBER OF SERVINGS 6

PER SERVING *296 cal., 0 g fat, 0 mg chol., 169 mg sodium, 51 g carb., 0 g fiber, 51 g sugars, 4 g pro.*

Prepare as directed. Cover and refrigerate up to 24 hours before cutting into cubes.

LEMON DROP MARTINI CUBES

PREP 15 minutes **CHILL** 3 hours

3 3-oz. pkg. lemon-flavor gelatin

2¾ cups boiling water

1 cup vodka

6 Tbsp. lemon juice

Nonstick cooking spray

Sugar and/or lemon slices

1. In a large bowl stir together lemon gelatin and boiling water until completely dissolved. Add vodka and lemon juice.

2. Coat a 3-qt. rectangular baking dish with cooking spray. Pour gelatin mixture into dish. Chill 3 hours or until firm. Cut into 1-inch squares. Serve in sugar-rimmed cocktail glasses with lemon slices.

NUMBER OF SERVINGS 6

PER SERVING *260 cal., 0 g fat, 0 mg chol., 244 mg sodium, 42 g carb., 0 g fiber, 41 g sugars, 4 g pro.*

Prepare as directed. Cover and refrigerate up to 24 hours before cutting into cubes.

**FRENCH TOAST
CASSEROLE WITH
CINNAMON-PEAR
COMPOTE**
Recipe on page 43

COFFEE CAKES & BREAKFAST BAKES

FRUIT COFFEE CAKE

PREP 35 minutes **BAKE** 45 minutes at 350°F

3 to 4 cups fresh blueberries;
fresh red raspberries;
sliced peeled apricots;
sliced peeled peaches;
and/or chopped peeled
apples

½ cup water

½ cup sugar

¼ cup cornstarch

3 cups all-purpose flour

1½ cups sugar

1 tsp. baking powder

½ tsp. baking soda

½ cup butter, cut up

2 eggs, lightly beaten

1 cup buttermilk or sour milk*

1 tsp. vanilla

½ cup all-purpose flour

½ cup sugar

¼ cup butter, cut up

1. For filling, in a medium saucepan combine fruit and the water. Bring to boiling; reduce heat. Cover and simmer 5 minutes or until fruit is tender. (Raspberries are a tender fruit and do not need to be simmered.) Combine ½ cup sugar and the cornstarch; stir into fruit. Cook and stir over medium heat until mixture is thickened and bubbly. Cook and stir 2 minutes more; set aside.

2. Preheat oven to 350°F. In a medium bowl combine the next four ingredients (through baking soda). Cut in the ½ cup butter until mixture resembles coarse crumbs. Make a well in the center of the flour mixture.

3. In another bowl combine eggs, buttermilk, and vanilla. Add egg mixture all at once to flour mixture. Stir just until moistened (batter should be lumpy). Spread half the batter into an ungreased 13×9-inch baking pan. Spoon and gently spread filling over batter. Drop remaining batter in small mounds onto filling.

4. In a bowl stir together the ½ cup flour and ½ cup sugar. Cut in the ¼ cup butter until mixture resembles coarse crumbs. Sprinkle over coffee cake. Bake 45 to 50 minutes or until golden. Cool slightly on a wire rack. Serve warm.

NUMBER OF SERVINGS 18

*TIP To make 1 cup sour milk, place 1 Tbsp. lemon juice or vinegar in a glass measuring cup. Add enough milk to equal 1 cup total liquid. Let stand 5 minutes before using.

PER SERVING *298 cal., 9 g fat (5 g sat. fat), 44 mg chol., 126 mg sodium, 52 g carb., 1 g fiber, 31 g sugars, 4 g pro.*

Cover cooled coffee cake with heavy foil. Store in the refrigerator up to 2 days or in the freezer up to 1 month. To serve, thaw coffee cake, if frozen. Reheat coffee cake, covered with foil, in a 300°F oven about 20 minutes.

STRAWBERRY-RHUBARB COFFEE CAKE

PREP 30 minutes **BAKE** 50 minutes at 350°F

1 orange

2 Tbsp. cornstarch

4 cups chopped rhubarb, thawed if frozen

1 cup sliced strawberries

½ cup granulated sugar

⅔ cup all-purpose flour

⅔ cup regular rolled oats

½ cup packed brown sugar

6 Tbsp. butter, cut up

2 cups all-purpose flour

1 cup whole wheat flour

1 Tbsp. baking powder

1 tsp. ground cardamom

½ tsp. baking soda

½ tsp. salt

1 cup butter, softened

1⅓ cups granulated sugar

4 eggs

1 16-oz. carton sour cream

1. Preheat oven to 350°F. Grease a 13×9-inch baking pan.

2. Remove 2 tsp. zest and squeeze 4 Tbsp. juice from orange. For filling, in a bowl combine 2 Tbsp. of the orange juice and the cornstarch. In a small saucepan combine rhubarb, strawberries, the ½ cup granulated sugar, and the remaining 2 Tbsp. orange juice. Bring to a simmer over medium heat, stirring occasionally. Cook 4 to 6 minutes or until rhubarb is tender, stirring often. Add the cornstarch mixture; cook 1 minute or until thickened, stirring constantly. Remove from heat. Cool completely.

3. For topping, in a bowl combine the ⅔ cup flour, the oats, and brown sugar. Using a pastry blender, cut in the 6 tablespoons butter until mixture resembles coarse crumbs.

4. For cake, in a bowl stir together the next six ingredients (through salt). In a large bowl beat the 1 cup butter with a mixer on medium to high for 30 seconds. Beat in the 1⅓ cups granulated sugar until fluffy. Add eggs, sour cream, and orange zest; beat until combined. Add flour mixture; beat on low just until combined.

5. Spread half the batter in the prepared baking pan. Spread cooled filling over batter. Spoon remaining batter in small mounds over filling. Sprinkle with topping.

6. Bake 50 to 55 minutes or until a toothpick comes out clean. Cover with foil the last 15 minutes to prevent overbrowning. Serve warm or cool.

NUMBER OF SERVINGS 20

PER SERVING *368 cal., 19 g fat (11 g sat. fat), 84 mg chol., 288 mg sodium, 47 g carb., 2 g fiber, 21 g sugars, 5 g pro.*

Prepare as directed through Step 5. Cover and refrigerate 4 to 24 hours. Bake as directed, but watch carefully. It may need to bake up to 15 minutes longer.

BANANA-COCONUT COFFEE CAKE WITH MACADAMIA NUT STREUSEL

PREP 30 minutes **BAKE** 35 minutes at 350°F **COOL** 30 minutes

3½ cups all-purpose flour

¾ cup flaked coconut

1 Tbsp. baking powder

1 tsp. baking soda

1 tsp. salt

1 cup butter, softened

¾ cup granulated sugar

¾ cup packed brown sugar

4 eggs

3 ripe bananas, mashed

¼ cup coffee liqueur or strong brewed coffee

¼ cup milk

2 tsp. vanilla

¼ cup all-purpose flour

¼ cup packed brown sugar

½ tsp. ground cinnamon

¼ cup butter, cut up

½ cup coarsely chopped macadamia nuts

1 recipe Powdered Sugar Icing

1. Preheat oven to 350°F. Grease and flour a 13×9-inch baking pan. In a bowl stir together the first five ingredients (through salt).

2. In an extra-large bowl beat the 1 cup butter, ¾ cup granulated sugar, and ¾ cup brown sugar with a mixer on medium to high until light and fluffy. Scrape sides of bowl; beat 1 minute. Add eggs, one at a time, beating well after each addition. Beat in bananas, liqueur, milk, and vanilla on low just until combined (mixture may appear curdled). Add flour mixture, beating on low just until combined. Spread batter into the prepared pan.

3. For streusel, in a bowl stir together the ¼ cup flour, ¼ cup brown sugar, and the cinnamon. Using a pastry blender, cut in the ¼ cup butter until mixture resembles coarse crumbs. Stir in macadamia nuts. Sprinkle evenly over top of batter.

4. Bake 35 to 40 minutes or until a toothpick comes out clean. Cool in pan on a wire rack 30 minutes. Drizzle with Powdered Sugar Icing. Serve warm.

NUMBER OF SERVINGS 18

POWDERED SUGAR ICING In a small bowl stir together ¾ cup powdered sugar, 4 tsp. milk, ½ tsp. vanilla, and, if desired, a few drops coconut extract until smooth.

PER SERVING *364 cal., 18 g fat (10 g sat. fat), 76 mg chol., 424 mg sodium, 45 g carb., 2 g fiber, 24 g sugars, 5 g pro.*

MAKE AHEAD

Cover cooled uniced coffee cake with heavy foil. Store in the refrigerator up to 2 days or freeze up to 1 month. To serve, thaw coffee cake, if frozen. Reheat coffee cake, covered with foil, in a 300°F oven about 20 minutes; drizzle with icing.

LEMON-FOLDOVERS COFFEE CAKE

PREP 50 minutes **STAND** 10 minutes **RISE** 1 hour 30 minutes **BAKE** 25 minutes at 350°F **COOL** 10 minutes

½ cup warm water
(105°F to 115°F)

1 pkg. active dry yeast

2 eggs, room temperature

⅓ cup buttermilk, room
temperature

⅓ cup granulated sugar

¼ cup butter, melted

1½ tsp. vanilla

½ tsp. salt

3½ to 4 cups all-purpose flour

½ cup granulated sugar

3 Tbsp. lemon zest

1 Tbsp. orange zest

½ cup lemon curd

¼ cup butter, melted

1 recipe Lemon-Cream
Cheese Icing

1. In a large bowl stir together the warm water and yeast. Let stand 10 minutes or until foamy. Lightly beat the eggs. Add eggs and the next five ingredients (through salt) to yeast mixture; mix well.

2. Gradually beat in 2½ cups of the flour with a mixer on low (dough will be soft and slightly sticky). Beat on low 5 minutes more. Stir in as much of the remaining flour as you can to make a moderately soft dough (dough will still be slightly sticky). Cover; let rise in a warm place until double in size (about 1 hour).

3. Meanwhile, combine the ½ cup granulated sugar, the lemon zest, and orange zest; mix well, pressing with the back of a spoon to release oils from zest. Line a 13×9-inch baking pan with foil, extending foil over edges of pan; grease foil.

4. Punch dough down. Turn dough out onto a lightly floured surface. Roll dough into an 18×12-inch rectangle. Cut into eighteen 4×3-inch rectangles. Spoon a slightly rounded teaspoon of lemon curd into the center of each rectangle. Moisten the edges with water. Fold in half diagonally to make triangles; press edges to seal.

5. Arrange the foldovers in the prepared pan in two lengthwise rows of nine, making sure sealed corners of the triangles point up. Drizzle with ¼ cup melted butter. Sprinkle with sugar mixture. Cover; let rise in a warm place until nearly double in size (about 30 minutes).

6. Preheat oven to 350°F. Bake 25 to 30 minutes or until golden. (If needed, cover with foil the last 10 minutes to prevent overbrowning.) Cool in pan on a wire rack 10 minutes. Use foil to lift coffee cake out of pan. Drizzle with Lemon-Cream Cheese Icing. Serve warm.

NUMBER OF SERVINGS 12

LEMON-CREAM CHEESE ICING In a bowl beat 2 oz. softened cream cheese, 1 Tbsp. milk, 1½ tsp. lemon juice, and ½ tsp. vanilla with a mixer on medium until smooth. Beat in 1¼ cups powdered sugar. If needed, beat in additional powdered sugar to make icing drizzling consistency.

PER SERVING *385 cal., 11 g fat (7 g sat. fat), 71 mg chol., 196 mg sodium, 66 g carb., 3 g fiber, 36 g sugars, 6 g pro.*

PEANUT BUTTER-BERRY BRUNCH CASSEROLE

PREP 30 minutes **CHILL** 2 hours **STAND** 30 minutes **BAKE** 40 minutes at 350°F **COOL** 10 minutes

2 Tbsp. butter

10 cups baguette bread cubes, dried

½ cup chunky natural peanut butter

1 8-oz. pkg. cream cheese, softened

2 tsp. granulated sugar

½ cup blackberry and/or strawberry jam

6 eggs

3½ cups milk

½ cup heavy cream

6 Tbsp. granulated sugar

1¼ tsp. vanilla

½ tsp. salt

¼ tsp. freshly grated nutmeg or ground nutmeg

3 Tbsp. butter, melted

¼ cup sugar cubes, coarsely crushed (optional)

Fresh blackberries and/or strawberries (optional)

1. Butter a 3-qt. rectangular baking dish. Arrange bread cubes in the prepared dish. In a bowl stir together peanut butter, half the cream cheese, and the 2 tsp. sugar. Use two spoons to drop mounds of peanut butter mixture into crevices among the bread cubes. Drop mounds of jam into empty crevices. Cube the remaining cream cheese and place cubes in any empty spaces.

2. In a large bowl whisk together the next seven ingredients (through nutmeg). Pour egg mixture over bread mixture in dish. Cover and chill at least 2 hours or overnight.

3. Let casserole stand at room temperature 30 minutes before baking. Preheat oven to 350°F. Uncover dish. Drizzle with butter and, if desired, sprinkle with crushed sugar cubes. Bake 40 to 45 minutes or until center is puffed and golden. If necessary, cover with foil the last 10 minutes to prevent overbrowning. Remove from oven. Cool on a wire rack 10 minutes before serving. If desired, sprinkle with fresh berries.

NUMBER OF SERVINGS 12

PER SERVING 427 cal., 24 g fat (11 g sat. fat), 141 mg chol., 529 mg sodium, 42 g carb., 2 g fiber, 19 g sugars, 13 g pro.

Natural peanut butter is a healthier choice than regular peanut butter because it has less saturated fat, sodium, and sugars. To reduce fat in this casserole, opt for light cream cheese over the full-fat version.

PEACHES AND CREAM BREAD PUDDING

PREP 25 minutes **CHILL** 8 hours **STAND** 15 minutes **BAKE** 40 minutes at 350°F

If you are lucky enough to have leftover caramel sauce, drizzle a little over ice cream, warm brownies, or grilled peaches. For a salty caramel treat, sprinkle with a pinch of kosher or coarse salt.

12 slices cinnamon swirl bread, halved diagonally

1 16-oz. pkg. frozen unsweetened peach slices, thawed, drained, and chopped

3 oz. cream cheese, cut into small cubes*

8 eggs, lightly beaten

2 cups milk

1 cup heavy cream

½ cup sugar

1 tsp. vanilla

½ tsp. salt

½ tsp. ground cinnamon

¼ tsp. ground nutmeg

1 recipe Caramel Sauce

½ cup coarsely chopped pecans, toasted (tip, page 21)

1. Arrange bread slices in an ungreased 3-qt. rectangular baking dish; top with peaches and cubed cream cheese. In a large bowl whisk together the next eight ingredients (through nutmeg). Pour egg mixture over bread mixture in dish. Using the back of a large spoon, press down lightly to moisten all ingredients. Cover and chill 8 to 24 hours.

2. Let bread pudding stand at room temperature 15 minutes before baking. Preheat oven to 350°F. Bake, uncovered, 40 to 50 minutes or until set.

3. Before serving, drizzle bread pudding with Caramel Sauce and sprinkle with pecans. Store any remaining sauce in the refrigerator up to 1 week.

NUMBER OF SERVINGS 12

CARAMEL SAUCE In a medium-size heavy saucepan stir together ¾ cup packed brown sugar, ½ cup heavy cream, ½ cup butter, and 2 Tbsp. light-color corn syrup. Bring to boiling over medium-high heat, whisking occasionally; reduce heat to medium. Boil gently 3 minutes more. Remove from heat. Stir in 1 tsp. vanilla. Let cool 15 minutes before serving.

*TIP To make cubing cream cheese easier, place it in the freezer 15 to 30 minutes.

PER SERVING *473 cal., 29 g fat (15 g sat. fat), 214 mg chol., 431 mg sodium, 45 g carb., 2 g fiber, 26 g sugars, 9 g pro.*

PUFFED OVEN PANCAKE WITH GLAZED APPLES

PREP 15 minutes **BAKE** 20 minutes at 400°F

Apples or bananas? Take your pick! If bananas are your preference, heat the brown sugar and butter together until melted, then stir in three sliced bananas. Stir them gently until heated, then add the rum.

2 Tbsp. butter

4 eggs

⅔ cup all-purpose flour

⅔ cup milk

¼ tsp. salt

½ cup butter, cut up

2 medium cooking apples, cored, peeled, and thinly sliced (about 2 cups)

⅓ cup packed brown sugar

2 Tbsp. light rum or apple juice

Powdered sugar (optional)

1. Preheat oven to 400°F. Place the 2 Tbsp. butter in a 13×9-inch baking pan. Place pan in oven 3 to 5 minutes or until butter is melted.

2. In a bowl beat eggs with a wire whisk. Whisk in flour, milk, and salt until smooth. Immediately pour batter into the hot pan. Bake 20 to 25 minutes or until puffed and well browned.

3. Meanwhile, for glazed apples, in a large skillet melt the ½ cup butter over medium heat; add apples. Cook and stir about 8 minutes or until apples are tender. Stir in brown sugar; cook 1 to 2 minutes or until sauce is smooth, stirring gently. Remove skillet from heat. Carefully stir in rum. Return skillet to heat; heat through.

4. Serve glazed apples over pancake. If desired, sprinkle lightly with powdered sugar. Serve warm.

NUMBER OF SERVINGS 8

PER SERVING *278 cal., 17 g fat (10 g sat. fat), 133 mg chol., 235 mg sodium, 24 g carb., 1 g fiber, 15 g sugars, 5 g pro.*

FRENCH TOAST CASSEROLE WITH CINNAMON-PEAR COMPOTE

PREP 30 minutes   **CHILL** 1 hour   **BAKE** 35 minutes at 375°F

Hearty whole wheat bread is the best choice for this bread-puddinglike dish. This French toast will soak up spoonfuls of the luscious pear compote.

5 eggs, lightly beaten

1 cup milk

⅓ cup granulated sugar

⅓ cup heavy cream

1 tsp. vanilla

¼ tsp. ground cinnamon

Dash salt

6 1-inch slices dried whole wheat bread*

1 Tbsp. granulated sugar

2 Tbsp. butter

2 cups sliced peeled pears

¼ cup water

2 Tbsp. granulated sugar

1 Tbsp. brandy (optional)

¼ tsp. ground cinnamon

Dash ground nutmeg

⅓ cup maple syrup

Powdered sugar (optional)

Whipped cream (optional)

1. For French toast, grease a 3-qt. rectangular baking dish. In a large shallow dish combine the first seven ingredients (through salt), stirring until sugar is dissolved. Dip bread slices into egg mixture, turning to coat both sides. Arrange dipped slices in the prepared baking dish. Cover and chill 1 to 24 hours.

2. Preheat oven to 375°F. Sprinkle bread slices with the 1 Tbsp. granulated sugar. Bake, uncovered, 35 minutes or until golden and puffed.

3. Meanwhile, in a medium saucepan melt butter over medium heat. Add the next six ingredients (through nutmeg). Cook and stir 5 minutes or just until pears are tender. Gently stir in maple syrup.

4. If desired, sprinkle French toast with powdered sugar. Serve with pear compote and, if desired, whipped cream.

NUMBER OF SERVINGS 6

*TIP To dry bread slices, arrange bread on a large baking sheet; cover loosely and let stand overnight. Or preheat oven to 300°F. Bake bread slices, uncovered, 5 minutes; cool.

PER SERVING *437 cal., 16 g fat (8 g sat. fat), 208 mg chol., 370 mg sodium, 63 g carb., 5 g fiber, 40 g sugars, 14 g pro.*

CHEESY POTATO BAKE WITH EGGS

PREP 35 minutes **BAKE** 55 minutes at 325°F

2 Tbsp. butter

½ cup finely chopped onion

4 tsp. all-purpose flour

1 tsp. salt

¾ tsp. black pepper

1½ cups milk

2 cups shredded sharp cheddar cheese (8 oz.)

3 lb. russet potatoes, peeled and thinly sliced*

1 Tbsp. vegetable oil

1½ cups chopped fresh or frozen broccoli

8 eggs

2 Tbsp. water

6 slices bacon, crisp-cooked, drained, and crumbled

1 large tomato, chopped

1. Preheat oven to 325°F. For cheese sauce, in a medium saucepan melt butter over medium heat. Add onion; cook about 4 minutes or until tender, stirring occasionally. Stir in flour, ½ tsp. of the salt, and ½ tsp. of the pepper. Stir in milk; cook and stir until slightly thickened and bubbly. Add cheese; stir until melted.

2. In a 3-qt. rectangular baking dish layer thinly sliced potatoes and cheese sauce. Bake, covered, about 55 minutes or until potatoes are tender.

3. In a large skillet heat oil over medium heat. Add broccoli; cook about 5 minutes or until crisp-tender, stirring frequently. In a large bowl beat together eggs, the water, and the remaining ½ tsp. salt and ¼ tsp. pepper. Pour over broccoli in skillet. Cook over medium heat, without stirring, until mixture begins to set on the bottom and around the edges. Using a spatula, lift and fold the partially cooked egg mixture so the uncooked portion flows underneath. Continue cooking about 2 minutes more or until egg mixture is cooked but still glossy and moist. Spoon eggs over potatoes. Top with bacon and chopped tomato. Serve immediately.

NUMBER OF SERVINGS 8

***TIP** To slice potatoes quickly, use a food processor fitted with a slicing blade or a mandoline slicer.

PER SERVING *421 cal., 22 g fat (11 g sat. fat), 259 mg chol., 708 mg sodium, 36 g carb., 3 g fiber, 7 g sugars, 21 g pro.*

FLEX IT

Have guests who don't eat meat? Serve this dish with crumbled bacon on the side, to be added or not.

FARMBOY CASSEROLE

PREP 25 minutes   **BAKE** 45 minutes at 350°F   **STAND** 5 minutes

Nonstick cooking spray

6 **cups frozen shredded hash brown potatoes**

1½ **cups shredded Monterey Jack cheese with jalapeño peppers or shredded cheddar cheese (6 oz.)**

2 **cups diced cooked ham, cooked breakfast sausage, or Canadian-style bacon**

½ **cup sliced green onions**

8 **eggs, lightly beaten**

3 **cups milk**

¼ **tsp. salt**

¼ **tsp. black pepper**

1. Preheat oven to 350°F. Coat a 3-qt. rectangular baking dish with cooking spray. Arrange hash brown potatoes evenly in the dish. Sprinkle with cheese, ham, and green onions.

2. In a bowl combine eggs, milk, salt, and pepper. Pour egg mixture over layers in dish.

3. Bake, uncovered, 45 to 55 minutes or until a knife inserted near the center comes out clean. Let stand 5 minutes before serving. If desired, sprinkle with additional sliced green onions.

NUMBER OF SERVINGS 12

PER SERVING *201 cal., 10 g fat (5 g sat. fat), 154 mg chol., 481 mg sodium, 11 g carb., 1 g fiber, 3 g sugars, 14 g pro.*

Prepare as directed through Step 2. Cover and refrigerate up to 24 hours. Preheat oven to 350°F. Bake, uncovered, 60 to 65 minutes or until a knife inserted near the center comes out clean.

It's easy to control fat in this hearty one-dish breakfast meal. Use reduced-fat cheddar cheese; 2 cups refrigerated or frozen egg product, thawed, for the whole eggs; and two 12-oz. cans evaporated fat-free milk for the milk.

EASY HUEVOS RANCHEROS CASSEROLE

PREP 15 minutes   **BAKE** 38 minutes at 375°F   **STAND** 10 minutes

Go retro with a tot-loaded casserole that appeals to any age. Set out bowls of salsa, sour cream, and cilantro to top individual servings.

Nonstick cooking spray

1 32-oz. pkg. frozen fried potato nuggets

12 eggs

1 cup milk

1½ tsp. dried oregano, crushed

1½ tsp. ground cumin

½ tsp. chili powder

¼ tsp. garlic powder

2 cups shredded Mexican-style four-cheese blend (8 oz.)

1 16-oz. jar thick and chunky salsa

1 8-oz. carton sour cream

Snipped fresh cilantro

1. Preheat oven to 375°F. Lightly coat a 3-qt. rectangular baking dish with cooking spray. Arrange potato nuggets in dish.

2. In a large bowl whisk together the next six ingredients (through garlic powder). Pour egg mixture over potato nuggets.

3. Bake, uncovered, 35 to 40 minutes or until a knife inserted near the center comes out clean. Sprinkle cheese over casserole. Bake 3 minutes more or until cheese is melted. Let stand 10 minutes before serving. Serve with salsa, sour cream, and cilantro.

NUMBER OF SERVINGS 12

PER SERVING *339 cal., 21 g fat (8 g sat. fat), 217 mg chol., 721 mg sodium, 22 g carb., 2 g fiber, 4 g sugars, 14 g pro.*

 FLEX IT

Add south-of-the-border kick by sprinkling cooked chorizo over the potato nuggets in the dish.

EGGS BENEDICT BAKE

PREP 25 minutes **BAKE** 25 minutes at 350°F

- 1 tsp. vinegar
- 8 eggs
- 4 English muffins, split
- ⅓ cup semisoft cheese with pepper, garlic, and herbs; garden vegetables; or toasted onion
- 8 thin slices cooked ham (12 oz.)
- 16 large fresh basil, spinach, or arugula leaves
- 8 thin slices tomato
- 1 recipe Shortcut Hollandaise Sauce

  Paprika and/or snipped fresh basil (optional)

1. Preheat broiler. Lightly grease an extra-large skillet. Fill skillet halfway with water; add vinegar. Bring to boiling; reduce heat to simmering (bubbles should begin to break the surface of the water). Break one of the eggs into a measuring cup. Holding the lip of the cup as close to the water as possible, carefully slip egg into simmering water. Repeat with the remaining seven eggs, allowing each egg an equal amount of space.

2. Simmer eggs, uncovered, 3 to 5 minutes or until whites are completely set and yolks begin to thicken but are not hard. Using a slotted spoon, remove eggs from skillet and place them in a large pan of warm water to keep warm.

3. Meanwhile, place muffin halves, cut sides up, on a baking sheet. Broil 3 to 4 inches from the heat about 2 minutes or until toasted; cool.

4. Grease a 3-qt. rectangular baking dish. Spread the cut side of each muffin half with about 2 tsp. of the cheese. Place muffin halves in the prepared baking dish. Top each with a slice of ham, folding or cutting to fit; two basil leaves; and a tomato slice.

5. Preheat oven to 350°F. Place cooked eggs on top of tomato slices. Spoon Shortcut Hollandaise Sauce over eggs. Bake, covered, about 25 minutes or until heated. If desired, sprinkle with paprika and/or snipped basil.

NUMBER OF SERVINGS 8

SHORTCUT HOLLANDAISE SAUCE In a bowl stir together ¾ cup each sour cream and mayonnaise, 2 Tbsp. lemon juice, and 1 Tbsp. Dijon-style mustard. If necessary, stir in milk, 1 tsp. at a time, to reach desired consistency.

PER SERVING *423 cal., 31 g fat (9 g sat. fat), 257 mg chol., 930 mg sodium, 17 g carb., 1 g fiber, 2 g sugars, 18 g pro.*

Start with Step 3 and prepare as directed through Step 4. Cover and refrigerate 2 to 24 hours. Prepare Shortcut Hollandaise Sauce; cover and refrigerate up to 24 hours. To serve, prepare eggs as directed in Steps 1 and 2. Continue as directed in Step 5.

GOAT CHEESE, ARTICHOKE, AND SMOKED HAM STRATA

PREP 30 minutes **STAND** 20 minutes **CHILL** 2 hours **BAKE** 1 hour at 350°F

2 cups whole milk

2 Tbsp. olive oil

1 1-lb. loaf sourdough bread, cut into 1-inch cubes (about 12 cups)

5 eggs

1½ cups half-and-half

1 Tbsp. minced garlic

1½ tsp. herbes de Provence

¾ tsp. black pepper

½ tsp. freshly ground nutmeg

½ tsp. dried sage, crushed

½ tsp. dried thyme, crushed

1 cup crumbled goat cheese (chèvre) (8 oz.)

12 oz. smoked ham, chopped

3 6-oz. jars marinated artichoke hearts, drained and halved lengthwise

1½ cups finely shredded Parmesan cheese (6 oz.)

1 cup shredded fontina cheese (4 oz.)

1. Preheat oven to 350°F. Grease a 3-qt. rectangular baking dish. In an extra-large bowl combine milk and olive oil. Add bread cubes, stirring to coat. Let stand 10 minutes.

2. In a large bowl whisk together the next eight ingredients (through thyme). Whisk in goat cheese until combined.

3. Spread half the bread cube mixture in the prepared dish. Top with half each of the ham, artichoke hearts, and cheeses. Repeat layers. Pour egg mixture over all. Cover and chill 2 to 24 hours.

4. Bake, uncovered, 1 hour or until center is set and edges are browned. Let stand 10 minutes before serving.

NUMBER OF SERVINGS 8

PER SERVING *693 cal., 38 g total fat (19 g sat. fat), 218 mg chol., 1,661 mg sodium, 47 g carb., 3 g fiber, 8 g sugar, 41 g pro.*

SPICY BRUNCH LASAGNA

PREP 40 minutes **CHILL** 8 hours **STAND** 35 minutes **BAKE** 1 hour at 350°F

1½ lb. bulk Italian sausage

1 24-oz. carton cottage cheese

½ cup finely chopped green onions

¼ cup snipped fresh chives

¼ cup finely shredded carrot

18 eggs

⅓ cup milk

½ tsp. salt

½ tsp. black pepper

2 Tbsp. butter

1 15- to 16-oz. jar Alfredo sauce

1 tsp. dried Italian seasoning, crushed

8 no-boil lasagna noodles

4 cups frozen shredded hash brown potatoes, thawed

2 cups shredded mozzarella cheese (8 oz.)

1. In a large skillet cook sausage until browned. Drain off fat. Meanwhile, in a bowl combine cottage cheese, green onions, chives, and carrot.

2. In an extra-large bowl whisk together eggs, milk, salt, and pepper. In a large skillet melt butter over medium heat. Add egg mixture. Cook, without stirring, until mixture begins to set on the bottom and around the edges. Using a spatula, lift and fold the partially cooked egg mixture so the uncooked portion flows underneath. Continue cooking 2 to 3 minutes more or until egg mixture is cooked but still glossy and moist. Remove from heat.

3. Stir together Alfredo sauce and Italian seasoning. Spread about ½ cup of the sauce in a 3-qt. rectangular baking dish. Layer half the lasagna noodles over sauce, overlapping as necessary. Top with half the remaining sauce, half the cottage cheese mixture, half the hash browns, half the scrambled egg mixture, and half the sausage mixture. Sprinkle with half the mozzarella cheese. Repeat layers.

4. Cover baking dish tightly with plastic wrap. Chill 8 to 24 hours.

5. Let lasagna stand at room temperature 30 minutes before baking. Preheat oven to 350°F. Remove plastic wrap; cover baking dish with foil. Bake 45 minutes. Remove foil. Bake about 15 minutes more or until heated through. Let stand 5 minutes before serving.

NUMBER OF SERVINGS 16

PER SERVING *452 cal., 30 g fat (12 g sat. fat), 290 mg chol., 918 mg sodium, 19 g carb., 1 g fiber, 2 g sugars, 24 g pro.*

It's easy to reduce the fat in this recipe. Look for Italian turkey sausage, low-fat cottage cheese, light Alfredo sauce, and part-skim mozzarella cheese to replace the higher-fat options.

**BACON-CARAMEL
ROLLS**
Recipe on page 59

SWEET & SAVORY SPIRALS

CINNAMON ROLLS

PREP 45 minutes **RISE** 1 hour 15 minutes **BAKE** 25 minutes at 375°F **COOL** 10 minutes

4¼ to 4¾ cups all-purpose flour

1 pkg. active dry yeast

1 cup milk

1 cup mashed cooked potato*

⅓ cup butter

⅓ cup granulated sugar

1 tsp. salt

2 eggs

½ cup packed brown sugar

1 Tbsp. ground cinnamon

¼ cup butter, softened

1 recipe Icing or Cream Cheese Icing

1. In a large bowl combine 1½ cups of the flour and the yeast. In a medium saucepan heat and stir the next five ingredients (through salt) just until warm (120°F to 130°F) and butter is almost melted; add to flour mixture along with the eggs. Beat with a mixer on low 30 seconds, scraping sides of bowl constantly. Beat on high 3 minutes. Stir in as much of the remaining flour as you can.

2. Turn dough out onto a lightly floured surface. Knead in enough remaining flour to make a moderately soft dough that is smooth and elastic (3 to 5 minutes total). Shape dough into a ball. Place in a lightly greased bowl; turn to grease surface of dough. Cover; let rise in a warm place until double in size (45 to 60 minutes).

3. Punch dough down. Turn out onto a lightly floured surface. Cover and let rest 10 minutes. Meanwhile, lightly grease a 13×9-inch baking pan. For filling, in a bowl stir together brown sugar and cinnamon.

4. Roll dough into an 18×12-inch rectangle. Spread the ¼ cup softened butter over dough and sprinkle with filling, leaving 1 inch unfilled along one long side. Starting from a long side, roll up rectangle into a spiral. Pinch dough to seal seams. Slice rolls into 12 pieces. Arrange pieces in the prepared pan. Cover and let rise in a warm place until nearly double in size (about 30 minutes).

5. Preheat oven to 375°F. Bake 25 to 30 minutes or until golden. Cool in pan on a wire rack 10 minutes. If desired, remove from pan. Drizzle or spread rolls with Icing. Serve warm.

NUMBER OF SERVINGS 12

ICING In a bowl stir together 1½ cups powdered sugar, ½ tsp. vanilla, and enough milk (4 to 6 tsp.) to reach drizzling consistency.

CREAM CHEESE ICING In a bowl beat 3 oz. softened cream cheese, 2 Tbsp. softened butter, and 1 tsp. vanilla with a mixer on medium until combined. Gradually beat in 2½ cups powdered sugar until smooth. Beat in milk, 1 tsp. at a time, to reach spreading consistency.

*TIP To make mashed potato, scrub a 10-oz. potato. Prick skin with a fork. Microwave 7 minutes or until tender. Halve potato and scoop pulp out of skin into a bowl; discard skin. Mash pulp. Measure 1 cup mashed potato.

PER ROLL *394 cal., 11 g fat (6 g sat. fat), 57 mg chol., 294 mg sodium, 68 g carb., 2 g fiber, 31 g sugars, 7 g pro.*

BACON-CARAMEL ROLLS

PREP 40 minutes **BAKE** 15 minutes at 400°F + 25 minutes at 375°F **RISE** 1 hour **COOL** 5 minutes

8 slices bacon

½ cup butter, melted

¾ cup packed brown sugar

¼ cup light-color corn syrup

¾ cup chopped pecans

⅔ cup packed brown sugar

1 Tbsp. ground cinnamon

2 16-oz. loaves frozen white bread dough or sweet roll dough, thawed

6 Tbsp. butter, softened

¾ cup raisins (optional)

1. Preheat oven to 400°F. Line a 15×10-inch baking pan with foil. Lay bacon in pan in a single layer. Bake about 15 minutes or until crisp; drain on paper towels. Coarsely chop bacon.

2. Grease a 13×9-inch baking pan. In a medium bowl stir together melted butter, the ¾ cup brown sugar, and the corn syrup. Stir in pecans and half the chopped bacon. Spread mixture in prepared pan.

3. Stir together the ⅔ cup brown sugar and the cinnamon. On a lightly floured surface, roll each loaf of dough into a 12×8-inch rectangle, stopping to let dough relax while rolling, if needed. Spread softened butter over dough rectangles. Sprinkle with brown sugar-cinnamon mixture, the remaining bacon, and, if desired, raisins.

4. Starting from a long side, roll up each rectangle into a spiral. Pinch dough to seal seams. Slice each roll into eight pieces. Arrange pieces in the prepared pan. Cover; let rise in a warm place until nearly double in size (about 1 hour).

5. Preheat oven to 375°F. Bake 25 to 30 minutes or until rolls are golden brown and sound hollow when gently tapped. If needed, cover rolls loosely with foil the last 10 minutes of baking to prevent overbrowning. Cool in pan on a wire rack 5 minutes. Invert rolls onto a platter. Serve warm.

NUMBER OF SERVINGS 16

PER ROLL *378 cal., 17 g fat (7 g sat. fat), 31 mg chol., 411 mg sodium, 51 g carb., 1 g fiber, 26 g sugars, 5 g pro.*

Cover baked and cooled rolls and refrigerate up to 3 days. Wrap rolls in foil and reheat in a 350°F oven 15 minutes. Or wrap in waxed paper and reheat, one at a time, in a microwave for 20 to 30 seconds or until warm.

CITRUS-HONEY SWEET ROLLS

PREP 45 minutes **STAND** 20 minutes **RISE** 1 hour 30 minutes **BAKE** 25 minutes at 350°F **COOL** 1 minute

1¼ cups warm water
  (105°F to 115°F)

2 pkg. active dry yeast

2 eggs, lightly beaten

½ cup nonfat dry milk powder

⅓ cup butter, softened

⅓ cup honey

2 tsp. ground cinnamon

2 Tbsp. toasted wheat germ

1 tsp. salt

2 cups bread flour

2½ to 3 cups white whole wheat
  flour or all-purpose flour

1 cup golden raisins
  (optional)

¼ cup butter, softened

¼ cup honey

2 tsp. lemon or orange zest

1 recipe Citrus Icing

Place iced rolls in an airtight container; cover. Store at room temperature up to 2 days. Or place uniced rolls in a freezer container; seal. Freeze up to 2 months. Thaw at room temperature before drizzling rolls with icing.

1. In a large bowl stir together the warm water and yeast; let stand about 5 minutes or until yeast is dissolved. Add the next six ingredients (through salt). Beat with a mixer on low to medium 30 seconds, scraping sides of bowl constantly. Add bread flour. Beat on low to medium 30 seconds more, scraping sides of bowl constantly. Beat on high 3 minutes. Stir in as much of the white whole wheat flour as you can.

2. Turn dough out onto a lightly floured surface. Knead in enough remaining white whole wheat flour to make a moderately soft dough that is smooth and elastic (3 to 5 minutes total). Shape dough into a ball. Place in a lightly greased bowl, turning once to grease surface of dough. Cover and let rise in a warm place until double in size (about 1 hour).

3. Punch dough down. Turn out onto a lightly floured surface. Cover and let rest 10 minutes. Meanwhile, lightly grease a 13×9-inch baking pan.

4. In a bowl combine raisins and enough warm water to cover. Let stand 5 minutes; drain well. For filling, in another bowl stir together the ¼ cup butter, ¼ cup honey, cinnamon, and lemon zest until smooth.

5. Roll dough into an 18×15-inch rectangle. Spread filling evenly over dough, leaving about 1 inch unfilled along the long sides. Sprinkle filling with raisins. Starting from a long side, roll up rectangle into a spiral. Pinch dough to seal seam. Slice roll into 15 pieces. Arrange pieces in the prepared baking pan. Cover and let rise in a warm place until nearly double in size (about 30 minutes).

6. Preheat oven to 350°F. Bake about 25 minutes or until golden. Cool in pan on a wire rack 1 minute. If desired, carefully invert rolls onto rack; cool slightly. Invert again onto a platter. Drizzle with Citrus Icing.

NUMBER OF SERVINGS 15

CITRUS ICING Remove 2 tsp. zest and squeeze 3 to 4 Tbsp. juice from 2 lemons. In a bowl combine 2 cups powdered sugar, the lemon zest, and 3 Tbsp. of the lemon juice. Stir in enough additional lemon juice to make drizzling consistency.

PER ROLL *363 cal., 8 g fat (5 g sat. fat), 45 mg chol., 252 mg sodium, 67 g carb., 3 g fiber, 36 g sugars, 8 g pro.*

CINNAMON-CHOCOLATE ROLLS
WITH HAZELNUTS

PREP 40 minutes   **RISE** 1 hour 15 minutes   **STAND** 10 minutes   **BAKE** 25 minutes at 375°F   **COOL** 10 minutes

3¾ to 4¼ cups unbleached
   all-purpose flour

1 pkg. active dry yeast

1 cup whole milk

⅔ cup sugar

¼ cup butter

1 tsp. salt

1 egg

1 cup purchased chocolate-
   hazelnut spread

¼ cup butter, melted

1 Tbsp. ground cinnamon

⅓ to ½ cup heavy cream

¼ cup hazelnuts, toasted*
   and chopped

1. In a large bowl stir together 1¼ cups of the flour and the yeast. In a medium saucepan heat and stir milk, ⅓ cup of the sugar, ¼ cup butter, and the salt just until warm (120°F to 130°F) and butter is almost melted. Add milk mixture to flour mixture; add egg. Beat with a mixer on low to medium 30 seconds, scraping sides of bowl constantly. Beat on high 3 minutes. Stir in as much remaining flour as you can.

2. Turn dough out onto a lightly floured surface. Knead in enough remaining flour to make a moderately soft dough that is smooth and elastic (3 to 5 minutes total). Shape dough into a ball. Place in a lightly greased bowl, turning once to grease surface of dough. Cover and let rise in a warm place until double in size (45 to 60 minutes).

3. Punch dough down. Turn out onto a lightly floured surface. Cover and let rest 10 minutes. Meanwhile, lightly grease a 13×9-inch baking pan. In a bowl combine ½ cup of the chocolate-hazelnut spread and the ¼ cup melted butter. In another bowl combine the remaining ⅓ cup sugar and the cinnamon.

4. Roll dough into a 15×10-inch rectangle. Spread chocolate-hazelnut mixture evenly over dough, leaving about ½ inch unfilled along the long sides. Sprinkle with cinnamon-sugar. Starting from a long side, roll up rectangle into a spiral. Pinch dough to seal seams. Slice roll into 12 pieces. Arrange pieces in the prepared baking pan. Cover and let rise in a warm place until nearly double in size (about 30 minutes).

5. Preheat oven to 375°F. Bake about 25 minutes or until golden. Cool in pan on wire rack 10 minutes. If desired, remove from pan.

6. For icing, in a small bowl combine the remaining ½ cup chocolate-hazelnut spread and ⅓ cup of the cream. If necessary, stir in additional cream, a small amount at a time, to reach drizzling consistency. Drizzle warm rolls with icing and sprinkle with hazelnuts. Serve warm.

***TIP** To toast hazelnuts, preheat oven to 350°F. Spread nuts in a shallow baking pan. Bake 8 to 10 minutes or until nuts are lightly toasted. Cool nuts slightly; place on a clean kitchen towel. Rub nuts with towel to remove loose skins.

NUMBER OF SERVINGS 12

PER ROLL *449 cal., 21 g fat (9 g sat. fat), 45 mg chol., 282 mg sodium, 58 g carb., 2 g fiber, 27 g sugars, 8 g pro.*

APPLE-CINNAMON ROLLS

PREP 50 minutes **RISE** 2 hours **STAND** 10 minutes **BAKE** 30 minutes at 375°F **COOL** 5 minutes

4½ to 5 cups all-purpose flour

1 pkg. active dry yeast

1 cup milk

⅓ cup butter

⅓ cup granulated sugar

½ tsp. salt

3 eggs

¾ cup packed brown sugar

¼ cup all-purpose flour

1 Tbsp. ground cinnamon or apple pie spice

½ cup butter, cut up

1¼ cups finely chopped peeled apples, ½ cup raisins, or ½ cup semisweet chocolate pieces

1 recipe Vanilla Frosting

MAKE AHEAD

Prepare as directed through Step 5, except do not let rise. Cover loosely with oiled waxed paper, then with plastic wrap. Chill 2 to 24 hours. Before baking, let chilled rolls stand, covered, at room temperature 30 minutes. Uncover and bake as directed. Or prepare, bake, and cool rolls as directed. Do not frost. Wrap in plastic wrap, then overwrap in foil. Freeze up to 2 months. To serve, thaw at room temperature. Spread or drizzle with Vanilla Frosting.

1. In a large bowl combine 2¼ cups of the flour and the yeast. In a small saucepan heat and stir the next four ingredients (through salt) just until warm (120°F to 130°F) and butter is almost melted. Add milk mixture to flour mixture; add eggs. Beat with a mixer on low to medium 30 seconds, scraping sides of bowl constantly. Beat on high 3 minutes. Stir in as much of the remaining 2¼ to 3¾ cups flour as you can.

2. Turn dough out onto a lightly floured surface. Knead in enough of the remaining flour to make a moderately soft dough that is smooth and elastic (3 to 5 minutes total). Shape dough into a ball. Place in a lightly greased bowl, turning once to grease surface. Cover and let rise in a warm place until double in size (1¼ to 1½ hours).

3. Punch dough down. Turn out onto a lightly floured surface. Cover and let rest 10 minutes. Meanwhile, lightly grease a 13×9-inch baking pan.

4. For filling, in a bowl stir together brown sugar, the ¼ cup flour, and the cinnamon. Using a pastry blender, cut in the ½ cup butter until mixture resembles coarse crumbs.

5. Roll dough into an 18×12-inch rectangle. Sprinkle with filling, leaving about 1 inch unfilled along one long side. Top with apples. Starting from a long side, roll up rectangle into a spiral. Pinch dough to seal seams. Slice into 12 pieces. Arrange pieces in the prepared baking pan. Cover and let rise in a warm place until nearly double in size (about 45 minutes).

6. Preheat oven to 375°F. Bake about 30 minutes or until golden, covering loosely with foil the last 10 minutes of baking. Cool in pan on a wire rack 5 minutes. If desired, remove from pan. Spread or drizzle with Vanilla Frosting. Serve warm.

NUMBER OF SERVINGS 12

VANILLA FROSTING In a bowl beat 1 cup powdered sugar, 2 Tbsp. each softened butter and milk, and 1 tsp. vanilla. Gradually beat in another 2 cups powdered sugar. If necessary, add additional milk, 1 tsp. at a time, to make a frosting of spreading or drizzling consistency.

PER ROLL *541 cal., 17 g fat (10 g sat. fat), 87 mg chol., 248 mg sodium, 90 g carb., 2 g fiber, 59 g sugars, 8 g pro.*

GINGERBREAD CINNAMON BUNS

PREP 30 minutes **STAND** 15 minutes **RISE** 1 hour 45 minutes **BAKE** 22 minutes at 350°F **COOL** 5 minutes

Add a little holiday cheer to these yeasty gingerbread rolls with a tumble of sugared cranberries. Simply roll frozen cranberries in granulated sugar.

¼ cup warm water
  (105°F to 115°F)

2 pkg. active dry yeast

½ cup evaporated milk

⅓ cup molasses

¼ cup packed brown sugar

1 egg, lightly beaten

2 Tbsp. vegetable oil

½ tsp. salt

3¾ to 4 cups all-purpose flour

¼ cup packed brown sugar

2 Tbsp. granulated sugar

1 tsp. ground cinnamon

½ tsp. ground ginger

¼ tsp. ground cloves

2 Tbsp. butter, softened

1 recipe Spiced Glaze

  Sugared cranberries
  (optional)

1. In a large bowl combine the warm water and yeast, stirring to dissolve yeast. Let stand 5 minutes. Stir in the next six ingredients (through salt). Stir in as much of the flour as you can.

2. Turn dough out onto a lightly floured surface. Knead in enough remaining flour to make a moderately soft dough that is smooth and elastic (3 to 5 minutes total). Shape dough into a ball. Place in a lightly greased bowl, turning once to grease surface. Cover and let rise in a warm place until double in size (1 to 1½ hours).

3. Punch down dough. Turn out onto a lightly floured surface. Cover and let stand 10 minutes. Lightly grease a 13×9-inch baking pan. For filling, combine the next five ingredients (through cloves).

4. Roll dough into a 12×8-inch rectangle. Spread dough with butter. Sprinkle with filling, leaving 1 inch unfilled along one long side. Starting from a long side, roll up rectangle into a spiral. Pinch dough to seal seams. Slice roll into 12 pieces. Arrange pieces in the prepared pan. Cover and let rise in a warm place until nearly double in size (about 45 minutes).

5. Preheat oven to 350°F. Bake 22 to 25 minutes or until golden brown. Cool in pan on a wire rack 5 minutes. If desired, remove from pan. Drizzle with Spiced Glaze. If desired, sprinkle with sugared cranberries. Serve warm.

NUMBER OF SERVINGS 12

SPICED GLAZE In a bowl stir together 1½ cups powdered sugar, 1 Tbsp. milk, ½ tsp. ground cinnamon, and ½ tsp. vanilla. Stir in additional milk, 1 tsp. at a time, to make glaze drizzling consistency.

PER ROLL *332 cal., 6 g fat (2 g sat. fat), 26 mg chol., 136 mg sodium, 64 g carb., 1 g fiber, 32 g sugars, 6 g pro.*

MAKE AHEAD

Place glazed rolls in an airtight container; cover. Store at room temperature up to 2 days. Or place unglazed rolls in a freezer container. Freeze up to 2 months. Thaw at room temperature before drizzling rolls with glaze.

FLORENTINE-FETA ROLLS

PREP 25 minutes   **BAKE** 18 minutes at 400°F   **COOL** 2 minutes

⅓ cup finely chopped green onions

¼ cup snipped fresh basil

2 cloves garlic, minced

2 Tbsp. olive oil

1 10-oz. pkg. frozen chopped spinach, thawed and squeezed dry

¼ tsp. black pepper

1 13.8-oz. pkg. refrigerated pizza dough

¼ cup crumbled feta cheese (1 oz.)

2 Tbsp. pine nuts, toasted (tip, page 21)

1 Tbsp. butter, melted

1. Preheat oven to 400°F. Grease the bottom of a 13×9-inch baking pan. In a large skillet cook and stir onions, basil, and garlic in 1 Tbsp. of the hot olive oil over medium heat for 1 to 2 minutes or until basil is wilted and onions are tender. Remove from heat. Stir in spinach and pepper.

2. On a well-floured surface, unroll pizza dough and shape into a 12×8-inch rectangle. Brush surface of dough with the remaining 1 Tbsp. olive oil. Spread spinach mixture to within 1 inch of the edges of dough. Sprinkle with feta cheese and pine nuts. Starting from a long side, roll up rectangle into a spiral. Pinch dough to seal seams. Slice roll into 12 pieces. Arrange pieces in the prepared pan. Brush with butter.

3. Bake 18 to 20 minutes or until golden brown. Let cool in pan on a wire rack 2 minutes. Remove from pan and serve warm.

NUMBER OF SERVINGS 12

PER ROLL 138 cal., 6 g fat (2 g sat. fat), 5 mg chol., 309 mg sodium, 17 g carb., 1 g fiber, 2 g sugars, 4 g pro.

PESTO ROLL-UPS

PREP 20 minutes **RISE** 30 minutes **BAKE** 20 minutes at 375°F

It takes only four ingredients to make these easy pesto spirals. Serve them with a small bowl of warm marinara sauce for dipping or alongside a pasta dish or cup of soup.

Nonstick cooking spray

1 16-oz. loaf frozen whole wheat bread dough, thawed

⅓ cup purchased basil pesto

⅓ cup bottled roasted red sweet peppers, drained, patted dry, and chopped

⅓ cup + 1 Tbsp. finely shredded Parmesan cheese

1. Coat a 13×9-inch baking pan with cooking spray. On a lightly floured surface, roll bread dough into a 12×8-inch rectangle. Spread pesto over dough to within 1 inch of long sides. Sprinkle roasted peppers and ⅓ cup of the cheese over pesto. Starting from a long side, roll up rectangle into a spiral. Pinch dough to seal seams. Slice roll into 12 pieces. Arrange pieces in the prepared pan. Cover; let rolls rise in a warm place until nearly double in size (30 to 45 minutes).

2. Preheat oven to 375°F. Uncover rolls and sprinkle with the remaining 1 Tbsp. cheese. Bake 20 to 25 minutes or until golden brown. If desired, spread with additional pesto. Immediately remove rolls from pan and serve warm.

NUMBER OF SERVINGS 12

PER ROLL *137 cal., 5 g fat (1 g sat. fat), 2 mg chol., 337 mg sodium, 19 g carb., 2 g fiber, 0 g sugars, 6 g pro.*

CHEESEBURGER SPIRALS

PREP 30 minutes **RISE** 1 hour 15 minutes **STAND** 10 minutes **BAKE** 35 minutes at 375°F **COOL** 5 minutes

These spirals are everything you love about cheeseburgers. Baked into a roll, there's no need to fire up the grill. Serve with the usual burger toppings: chopped onion, ketchup, mustard, and pickles.

4½ to 5 cups all-purpose flour

1 pkg. active dry yeast

1 cup milk

1 cup mashed cooked potato (tip, page 56)

⅓ cup butter, cut up

3 Tbsp. sugar

1 tsp. salt

2 eggs

1 lb. extra-lean ground beef

½ cup finely chopped onion

½ tsp. salt

½ tsp. black pepper

⅓ cup ketchup

¼ cup yellow mustard

¼ cup chopped dill pickles

1 cup shredded sharp cheddar cheese (4 oz.)

Sesame seeds (optional)

1. In a large bowl combine 1½ cups of the flour and the yeast. In a saucepan heat and stir the next five ingredients (through salt) just until warm (120°F to 130°F) and butter is almost melted; add to flour mixture along with the eggs. Beat with a mixer on low 30 seconds, scraping sides of bowl. Beat on high 3 minutes. Stir in as much remaining flour as you can.

2. Turn dough out onto a lightly floured surface. Knead in enough remaining flour to make a moderately soft dough that is smooth and elastic (3 to 5 minutes total). Shape dough into a ball. Place in a lightly greased bowl; turn once to grease surface. Cover; let rise in a warm place until double in size (45 to 60 minutes).

3. Meanwhile, in a large skillet cook beef, onion, the ½ tsp. salt, and the pepper over medium heat until beef is browned; drain. Stir in ketchup and mustard.

4. Punch down dough. Turn out onto a lightly floured surface. Cover; let rest 10 minutes. Lightly grease a 13×9-inch baking pan.

5. Roll dough into an 18×12-inch rectangle. Top evenly with beef mixture, pickles, and cheese, leaving 1 inch unfilled along one long side. Starting from a long side, roll up rectangle into a spiral. Pinch dough to seal seams. Slice roll into 12 pieces. Arrange pieces in the prepared pan. If desired, sprinkle with sesame seeds. Cover; let rise in a warm place until nearly double in size (about 30 minutes).

6. Preheat oven to 375°F. Bake about 35 minutes or until a thermometer inserted near the center registers 200°F, covering with foil the last 10 minutes, if necessary, to prevent overbrowning. Cool in pan on a wire rack 5 minutes. If desired, remove from pan. Serve warm.

NUMBER OF SERVINGS 12

PER ROLL *374 cal., 13 g fat (7 g sat. fat), 79 mg chol., 584 mg sodium, 46 g carb., 2 g fiber, 6 g sugars, 18 g pro.*

BARBECUE CHICKEN SPIRALS

PREP 30 minutes   **RISE** 1 hour 15 minutes   **STAND** 10 minutes   **BAKE** 35 minutes at 375°F   **COOL** 5 minutes

4¼ to 4¾ cups all-purpose flour

1 pkg. active dry yeast

1 cup milk

1 cup mashed cooked sweet potato*

⅓ cup butter, cut up

3 Tbsp. packed brown sugar

1 tsp. salt

1 tsp. smoked paprika

1 tsp. chili powder

2 eggs

2½ cups shredded cooked chicken

½ cup barbecue sauce

⅓ cup sliced green onions

1 cup shredded Monterey Jack cheese with jalapeño peppers (4 oz.)

1. In a large bowl combine 1½ cups of the flour and the yeast. In a saucepan heat and stir the next seven ingredients (through chili powder) just until warm (120°F to 130°F); add to flour mixture along with the eggs. Beat with a mixer on low 30 seconds, scraping sides of bowl. Beat on high 3 minutes. Stir in as much remaining flour as you can.

2. Turn dough out onto a lightly floured surface. Knead in enough remaining flour to make a moderately soft dough that is smooth and elastic (3 to 5 minutes total). Shape dough into a ball. Place in a lightly greased bowl; turn once to grease surface. Cover; let rise in a warm place until double in size (45 to 60 minutes).

3. Meanwhile, stir together chicken and barbecue sauce.

4. Punch down dough. Turn out onto a lightly floured surface. Cover; let rest 10 minutes. Lightly grease a 13×9-inch baking pan.

5. Roll dough into an 18×12-inch rectangle. Spread chicken mixture over dough, leaving 1 inch unfilled along one long side. Sprinkle with onions and cheese. Starting from a long side, roll up rectangle into a spiral. Pinch dough to seal seams. Slice roll into 12 pieces. Arrange pieces in the prepared pan. Cover; let rise in a warm place until nearly double in size (about 30 minutes).

6. Preheat oven to 375°F. Bake about 35 minutes or until a thermometer inserted near the center registers 200°F, covering with foil during the last 10 minutes of baking. Cool in pan on a wire rack 5 minutes; remove from pan. Serve warm. If desired, serve with additional barbecue sauce and sprinkle with additional green onions.

NUMBER OF SERVINGS 12

*TIP To make mashed sweet potato, scrub a 10-oz. potato. Prick skin with a fork. Microwave about 7 minutes or until tender. Halve potato and scoop pulp out of skin into a bowl; discard skin. Mash pulp. Measure 1 cup mashed potato.

PER ROLL *375 cal., 12 g fat (6 g sat. fat), 80 mg chol., 463 mg sodium, 48 g carb., 2 g fiber, 10 g sugars, 17 g pro.*

FLEX IT

If chicken isn't your meat choice for barbecue, use shredded smoked pork or beef and sharp cheddar cheese.

STROMBOLI SPIRALS

PREP 20 minutes **BAKE** 20 minutes at 375°F **COOL** 5 minutes

Stromboli is a baked stuffed pastry that is sliced to eat as a knife-and-fork entree. This handheld twist on the classic pairs perfectly with soup or goes solo as a snack or light lunch.

Nonstick cooking spray

1 13.8-oz. pkg. refrigerated pizza dough with whole grain

½ cup pizza sauce

½ cup chopped green sweet pepper

3 oz. thin slices deli-style turkey breast

3 oz. thin slices deli-style capicola

1½ cups shredded Italian-blend cheeses (6 oz.)

1. Preheat oven to 375°F. Grease a 13×9-inch baking pan with cooking spray. On a lightly floured surface, unroll pizza dough and stretch into a 12×10-inch rectangle. Spread pizza sauce over dough. Top with sweet pepper, turkey and capicola slices, and 1 cup of the cheese.

2. Starting from a long side, roll up rectangle into a spiral. Pinch dough to seal seams. Slice roll into 12 pieces. Arrange pieces in the prepared pan.

3. Bake 15 minutes. Sprinkle with the remaining ½ cup cheese. Bake about 5 minutes more or until golden and cheese is melted. Cool in pan on a wire rack 5 minutes. Remove from pan. If desired, serve with additional pizza sauce.

NUMBER OF SERVINGS 12

PER ROLL *175 cal., 8 g fat (3 g sat. fat), 20 mg chol., 526 mg sodium, 17 g carb., 1 g fiber, 2 g sugars, 10 g pro.*

FLEX IT

Mix and match a variety of sliced Italian deli meats, such as salami, mortadella, prosciutto, or sopressata, for the turkey and capicola.

REUBEN SPIRALS

PREP 25 minutes **RISE** 1 hour 30 minutes **STAND** 10 minutes **BAKE** 35 minutes at 375°F **COOL** 5 minutes

3¾ to 4¼ cups bread flour

1 pkg. active dry yeast

2 cups warm water (120°F to 130°F)

¼ cup packed brown sugar

2 Tbsp. vegetable oil

1 tsp. salt

1½ cups rye flour

1 Tbsp. caraway seeds

1 cup shredded Swiss cheese (4 oz.)

1 cup sauerkraut, rinsed and well-drained

6 oz. sliced corned beef or pastrami, chopped

Thousand Island dressing

1. In a large bowl stir together 2¾ cups of the bread flour and the yeast. Add the warm water, brown sugar, oil, and salt. Beat with a mixer on low to medium 30 seconds, scraping sides of bowl constantly. Beat on high 3 minutes. Stir in rye flour, caraway seeds, and as much remaining bread flour as you can.

2. Turn dough out onto a lightly floured surface. Knead in enough remaining bread flour to make a moderately stiff dough that is smooth and elastic (6 to 8 minutes total). Shape dough into a ball. Place in a lightly greased bowl; turn once to grease surface. Cover; let rise in a warm place until double in size (about 1 hour).

3. Punch dough down. Turn dough out onto a lightly floured surface. Cover; let rest 10 minutes. Meanwhile, lightly grease a 13×9-inch baking pan. Roll dough into an 18×12-inch rectangle. Sprinkle with cheese, sauerkraut, and corned beef, leaving 1 inch unfilled along one long side. Starting from a long side, roll up rectangle into a spiral. Pinch dough to seal seams. Slice roll into 12 pieces. Arrange pieces in the prepared pan. Cover; let rise in a warm place until nearly double in size (about 30 minutes).

4. Preheat oven to 375°F. Bake about 35 minutes or until a thermometer inserted near the center registers 200°F. Cool in pan on a wire rack 5 minutes; remove from pan. Serve warm with Thousand Island dressing.

NUMBER OF SERVINGS 12

PER ROLL *375 cal., 15 g fat (4 g sat. fat), 27 mg chol., 601 mg sodium, 49 g carb., 3 g fiber, 8 g sugars, 12 g pro.*

**TORTELLINI-
VEGETABLE BAKE**
Recipe on page 96

HEALTHY COMFORT FOOD

RAVIOLI LASAGNA WITH BABY KALE AND ITALIAN SAUSAGE

PREP 25 minutes **BAKE** 55 minutes at 375°F

- 1 5- to 6-oz. pkg. baby kale, coarsely chopped
- 12 oz. Italian-flavor cooked chicken sausage, chopped
- 1½ cups shredded mozzarella cheese (6 oz.)
- ½ cup snipped fresh basil
- 1 28-oz. can no-salt-added crushed tomatoes
- 1 14.5-oz. can fire-roasted diced tomatoes with garlic, undrained
- 1 8-oz. can no-salt-added tomato sauce
- 1 tsp. dried Italian seasoning, crushed
- ½ tsp. fennel seeds, crushed
- 2 9-oz. pkg. refrigerated cheese-filled ravioli
- Grated Parmesan cheese (optional)

1. Preheat oven to 375°F. Grease a 3-qt. rectangular baking dish. In a bowl combine kale, sausage, ¾ cup of the mozzarella cheese, and the basil. For sauce, in another bowl combine the next five ingredients (through fennel seeds).

2. Spread about 1 cup of the sauce in the prepared dish. Top with one package ravioli and half the kale mixture. Spoon another 1 cup sauce over kale mixture. Top with remaining ravioli and kale mixture. Spoon remaining sauce on top. Sprinkle with remaining ¾ cup mozzarella cheese.

3. Cover with nonstick or greased foil. Bake 30 minutes. Remove foil; bake 25 minutes more or until heated. If desired, top with Parmesan cheese and additional basil.

NUMBER OF SERVINGS 8

PER SERVING *378 cal., 13 g fat (7 g sat. fat), 82 mg chol., 858 mg sodium, 40 g carb., 6 g fiber, 10 g sugars, 24 g pro.*

Go meatless while keeping the Italian flavors in this lasagna. Swap one 15-oz. can cannellini beans, rinsed and drained, for the sausage.

CHICKEN ALFREDO CAULIFLOWER RICE BAKE

PREP 20 minutes **BAKE** 35 minutes at 400°F

Cauliflower chopped in the food processor is a low-carb alternative to rice. Look for orange, green, or purple varieties to make this dish pop with color.

- 1 2¼- to 2½-lb. head cauliflower, trimmed and broken into florets
- ¼ cup olive oil
- 1 tsp. dried basil, crushed
- ¼ tsp. salt
- ¼ tsp. black pepper
- 2½ cups fresh baby spinach
- 2 cups chopped rotisserie chicken
- 1 14.5-oz. jar light Alfredo pasta sauce
- 2 Tbsp. grated Parmesan cheese
- ½ cup panko bread crumbs

1. Preheat oven to 400°F. Working in batches, cover and pulse cauliflower in a food processor four to six times or until crumbly and resembles rice.

2. Transfer cauliflower "rice" to a 3-qt. rectangular baking dish or casserole. Drizzle with 2 Tbsp. of the oil and sprinkle with basil, salt, and pepper; toss to coat. Bake, uncovered, 15 minutes.

3. Stir in spinach, chicken, and pasta sauce; sprinkle with cheese. Stir together panko and the remaining 2 Tbsp. oil; sprinkle over cauliflower mixture. Bake 20 to 25 minutes more or until top is browned.

NUMBER OF SERVINGS 6

PER SERVING *255 cal., 16 g fat (6 g sat. fat), 83 mg chol., 743 mg sodium, 12 g carb., 2 g fiber, 3 g sugars, 17 g pro.*

CREAMY CHICKEN ENCHILADAS

PREP 50 minutes   **BAKE** 1 hour 5 minutes at 350°F   **STAND** 5 minutes

1 lb. skinless, boneless chicken breast halves

1 10-oz. pkg. frozen chopped spinach, thawed and well drained

½ cup thinly sliced green onions

1 16-oz. carton light sour cream

2 4-oz. cans diced green chiles, drained

1 cup milk

½ cup plain yogurt

¼ cup all-purpose flour

½ tsp. salt

½ tsp. ground cumin

12 7-inch flour tortillas

⅔ cup shredded Monterey Jack and/or cheddar cheese

Fresh cilantro sprigs (optional)

Salsa (optional)

1. Preheat oven to 350°F. In a large covered saucepan cook chicken in enough boiling water to cover for 12 to 14 minutes or until done (165°F); drain. Shred chicken using two forks.

2. In a bowl combine shredded chicken, spinach, and green onions. For sauce, in another bowl combine next seven ingredients (through cumin). Divide in half.

3. For filling, combine chicken mixture and one portion of the sauce. Spoon filling just below centers of tortillas; roll up tortillas. Place, seam sides down, in a 3-qt. rectangular baking dish. Spoon remaining sauce over tortillas.

4. Bake, covered, 65 to 70 minutes or until heated. Sprinkle with cheese. Let stand 5 minutes before serving. If desired, top with cilantro and/or additional green onions and serve with salsa.

NUMBER OF SERVINGS 12

PER ENCHILADA *270 cal., 10 g fat (5 g sat. fat), 49 mg chol., 518 mg sodium, 26 g carb., 2 g fiber, 2 g sugars, 17 g pro.*

Prepare as directed through Step 3, except do not spoon remaining sauce over tortillas. Cover dish and remaining sauce; refrigerate 2 to 24 hours. Continue as directed, spooning sauce over before baking.

TURKEY DINNER SHEPHERD'S PIE

PREP 45 minutes **BAKE** 25 minutes at 375°F

Shepherd's pie is designed to use leftover meat and vegetables. Traditionally topped with mashed russet potatoes, the addition of sweet potatoes in this recipe adds color and nutrients.

1½ lb. sweet potatoes, peeled and cut into 2-inch pieces

1½ lb. Yukon gold or other yellow-flesh potatoes, peeled and cut into 2-inch pieces

4 cloves garlic, halved

½ cup milk

½ tsp. salt

½ cup finely shredded Parmesan cheese (2 oz.)

2 Tbsp. olive oil

1½ cups chopped carrots

1 cup chopped red sweet pepper

1 cup chopped onion

3 cups chopped or shredded cooked turkey or chicken*

2 10.75-oz. cans condensed cream of mushroom soup

2 cups frozen cut green beans

½ cup dried cranberries

¼ cup water

3 Tbsp. Worcestershire sauce

1 Tbsp. snipped fresh sage or 1 tsp. dried sage, crushed

1 tsp. dry mustard

½ tsp. black pepper

1. Preheat oven to 375°F. In a 4-qt. covered Dutch oven cook potatoes and garlic in enough lightly salted boiling water to cover for 20 to 25 minutes or until tender; drain. Return potatoes to Dutch oven and mash. Gradually beat in milk and salt to make potatoes light and fluffy. Stir in cheese. Cover and keep warm.

2. Meanwhile, in a large skillet heat oil over medium heat. Add carrots, sweet pepper, and onion; cook until tender, stirring occasionally. Stir in the remaining ingredients; heat through. Transfer turkey mixture to a 3-qt. rectangular baking dish. Pipe or spoon mashed potatoes in 10 to 12 mounds on turkey mixture.

3. Bake, uncovered, 25 to 30 minutes or until heated through. If desired, top with additional fresh sage.

NUMBER OF SERVINGS 10

TIP If you don't have leftover turkey or chicken, remove and discard the skin and bones from a rotisserie chicken. Chop or shred the chicken meat.

PER SERVING *335 cal., 10 g fat (3 g sat. fat), 36 mg chol., 719 mg sodium, 43 g carb., 5 g fiber, 12 g sugars, 19 g pro.*

TACOS IN PASTA SHELLS

PREP 40 minutes **BAKE** 30 minutes at 350°F

These shells are certain to be a potluck favorite. Cover the dish tightly and transport it in an insulated carrier. Pack the tomato and olives separately in a cooler with ice packs.

24 dried jumbo macaroni shells

1½ lb. extra-lean ground beef

2½ cups salsa

4 oz. reduced-fat cream cheese (neufchatel), cut up

1 tsp. chili powder

1 cup shredded reduced-fat cheddar cheese (4 oz.)

Chopped tomato (optional)

Sliced pitted ripe olives (optional)

1. Cook shells according to package directions; drain. Rinse with cold water; drain again.

2. Meanwhile, preheat oven to 350°F. In an extra-large skillet cook ground beef over medium-high heat until browned. Drain off fat. Stir in 1 cup of the salsa, the cream cheese, and chili powder. Remove from heat; cool slightly. Fill cooked shells with meat mixture.

3. Spread 1 cup of the salsa in an ungreased 3-qt. rectangular baking dish. Arrange filled shells in baking dish; top with the remaining ½ cup salsa.

4. Bake, covered, 15 minutes. Sprinkle with cheddar cheese. Bake, uncovered, about 15 minutes more or until heated through. If desired, sprinkle with tomato and olives.

NUMBER OF SERVINGS: 8

PER SERVING *307 cal., 11 g fat (5 g sat. fat), 67 mg chol., 710 mg sodium, 28 g carb., 3 g fiber, 5 g sugars, 25 g pro.*

BEEF STROGANOFF CASSEROLE

PREP 35 minutes **BAKE** 20 minutes at 350°F

- 4 cups dried campanelle or penne pasta (12 oz.)
- 1 15-oz. pkg. refrigerated cooked beef roast au jus
- 2 large portobello mushrooms
- 1 medium sweet onion, cut into thin wedges
- 2 cloves garlic, minced
- ¼ cup butter
- ⅓ cup all-purpose flour
- ¼ cup tomato paste
- 2 14-oz. can 50% less sodium beef broth
- 2 Tbsp. Worcestershire sauce
- 2 tsp. smoked paprika or Spanish paprika
- ¼ tsp. salt
- ¼ tsp. black pepper
- Snipped fresh Italian parsley (optional)
- ½ cup sour cream
- 1 Tbsp. prepared horseradish
- 1 tsp. snipped fresh dill weed or ¼ tsp. dried dill weed

1. Preheat oven to 350°F. Cook pasta according to package directions; drain. Return pasta to hot pan; cover and keep warm. Place roast on a cutting board; reserve juices. Shred beef into bite-size pieces using two forks.

2. Remove stems and gills from mushrooms; coarsely chop. (You should have about 4 cups.) In an extra-large skillet cook mushrooms, onion, and garlic in hot butter over medium heat for 4 to 5 minutes or until tender. Stir in flour and tomato paste. Add reserved meat juices and the next five ingredients (through pepper). Cook and stir until thickened and bubbly. Remove from heat. Stir pasta and beef into mushroom mixture. Transfer stroganoff to a 3-qt. rectangular baking dish or casserole.

3. Bake, covered, 20 minutes or until heated. If desired, sprinkle with parsley. In a bowl stir together sour cream, horseradish, and dill. Serve with beef stroganoff.

NUMBER OF SERVINGS 6

PER SERVING *483 cal., 16 g fat (9 g sat. fat), 65mg chol., 831 mg sodium, 62 g carb., 4 g fiber, 10 g sugars, 24 g pro.*

PORK AND SQUASH ENCHILADAS

PREP 25 minutes **BAKE** 25 minutes at 350°F

1 to 2 Tbsp. olive oil

1 lb. pork tenderloin, cut into small pieces

1 small onion, halved lengthwise and thinly sliced

1 10-oz. can diced tomatoes and green chiles, drained

1 tsp. chili powder

1 14-oz. can mild enchilada sauce (about 1⅔ cups)

12 6-inch corn tortillas

1 12-oz. pkg. frozen cooked winter squash, thawed

2 cups shredded Mexican-style four-cheese blend (8 oz.)

Light sour cream, salsa, and/or cilantro leaves (optional)

1. Preheat oven to 350°F. In a large nonstick skillet heat 1 Tbsp. olive oil over medium heat. Add pork; cook and stir. Add onion slices and additional oil, if necessary. Add tomatoes and chili powder; cook and stir 2 minutes.

2. Pour ⅓ cup of the enchilada sauce into a 3-qt. rectangular baking dish; tilt dish to coat bottom with sauce. Stack tortillas and wrap in damp paper towels. Microwave about 40 seconds or until warm and soft. Top a tortilla with a slightly rounded tablespoon of the squash, about ¼ cup of the pork mixture, and 1 Tbsp. of the cheese. Roll up; place seam-side down in the prepared baking dish. Repeat with remaining tortillas. Pour remaining sauce over enchiladas and sprinkle with remaining cheese.

3. Bake, covered, about 25 minutes or until heated through and cheese is melted. If desired, serve with sour cream, salsa, and/or cilantro.

NUMBER OF SERVINGS 6

PER 2 ENCHILADAS *397 cal., 18 g fat (8 g sat. fat), 85 mg chol., 893 mg sodium, 31 g carb., 5 g fiber, 7 g sugars, 29 g pro.*

FLEX IT

For a meatless meal, substitute one or two 15-oz. cans pinto or black beans, rinsed and drained, for the pork. If desired, mash half the beans.

TUNA-NOODLE CASSEROLE

PREP 30 minutes **BAKE** 25 minutes at 375°F **STAND** 5 minutes

- 6 cups dried wide noodles (about 10 oz.)
- ½ cup butter, cut up
- 2 cups chopped red sweet peppers
- 1 cup chopped celery
- ½ cup chopped onion
- ½ cup all-purpose flour
- 2 to 3 Tbsp. Dijon-style mustard
- ½ tsp. salt
- ½ tsp. black pepper
- 4½ cups fat-free milk
- 2 12-oz. cans chunk white tuna (water pack), drained and broken into chunks, or four 5-oz. pouches chunk light tuna in water, drained
- 1 cup panko bread crumbs
- ½ cup grated Parmesan cheese
- 2 Tbsp. snipped fresh parsley
- 2 Tbsp. butter, melted

1. Preheat oven to 375°F. Lightly grease a 3-qt. rectangular baking dish. In a pot cook noodles according to package directions. Drain; return noodles to pot.

2. Meanwhile, for sauce, in a large saucepan melt butter over medium heat. Add sweet peppers, celery, and onion; cook 8 to 10 minutes or until tender, stirring occasionally. Stir in flour, mustard, salt, and black pepper. Add milk all at once; cook and stir until slightly thickened and bubbly.

3. Gently fold sauce and tuna into cooked noodles. Transfer noodle mixture to the prepared baking dish. In a bowl stir together the remaining ingredients. Sprinkle crumb mixture over casserole.

4. Bake, uncovered, 25 to 30 minutes or until heated through. Let stand 5 minutes before serving.

NUMBER OF SERVINGS 8

PER SERVING *486 cal., 20 g fat (11 g sat. fat), 113 mg chol., 779 mg sodium, 47 g carb., 3 g fiber, 11 g sugars, 28 g pro.*

FLEX IT

This classic casserole is easily adaptable. Instead of tuna, use four 6-oz. cans skinless, boneless salmon, drained; 2 cups shredded cooked chicken breast; or 2 cups julienned low-sodium ham.

ZOODLE PIZZA CASSEROLE

PREP 30 minutes **STAND** 15 minutes **BAKE** 25 minutes at 400°F

Not into gadgets? If you don't have a spiralizer, julienne cutter, or mandoline, coarsely shred the zucchini, or halve the zucchini lengthwise and cut it crosswise into ¼-inch slices.

Nonstick cooking spray

3 10- to 12-oz. zucchini

1½ tsp. kosher salt

2 eggs, lightly beaten

2 cups shredded mozzarella cheese (8 oz.)

¼ cup grated Parmesan cheese

¼ cup all-purpose flour

2 Tbsp. cornmeal

1 8-oz. can pizza sauce

½ cup miniature sliced pepperoni

1. Preheat oven to 400°F. Coat a 3-qt. rectangular baking dish with cooking spray. Using a vegetable spiralizer, julienne cutter, or mandoline, cut zucchini into long, thin noodles (zoodles). Place in a colander set in a sink and sprinkle with salt; toss gently. Let stand 15 minutes. Pat dry with paper towels.

2. In a bowl combine eggs, ½ cup of the mozzarella cheese, the Parmesan cheese, flour, and cornmeal. Stir in zoodles. Transfer to the prepared baking dish.

3. Bake, uncovered, 10 minutes or until set and no excess liquid remains. Spread pizza sauce over zoodle mixture. Top with remaining 1½ cups mozzarella cheese and the pepperoni. Bake 15 to 20 minutes more or until cheese is melted and casserole is heated through.

NUMBER OF SERVINGS 8

PER SERVING *191 cal., 10 g fat (5 g sat. fat), 75 mg chol., 678 mg sodium, 12 g carb., 2 g fiber, 4 g sugars, 13 g pro.*

FLEX IT

Skip the pepperoni but keep the flavor zesty by topping the casserole with finely chopped red sweet pepper and sliced pepperoncini salad peppers.

ROASTED CAULIFLOWER MAC AND CHEESE

PREP 40 minutes **ROAST** 20 minutes at 400°F **BAKE** 25 minutes at 350°F

- 6 cups small cauliflower florets
- 2 tsp. olive oil
- ¼ tsp. salt
- 2 cups dried elbow macaroni or cavatappi pasta
- 1 Tbsp. olive oil
- ¾ cup finely chopped onion
- 2 cloves garlic, minced
- 2½ cups fat-free milk
- 2 Tbsp. all-purpose flour
- ½ tsp. salt
- 2 oz. reduced-fat cream cheese (neufchatel), cut up
- 1½ cups shredded reduced-fat sharp cheddar cheese (6 oz.)
- 1 cup soft bread crumbs
- ¼ cup grated Parmesan cheese
- ½ tsp. snipped fresh thyme
- 1 tsp. olive oil

1. Preheat oven to 400°F. Line a 15×10-inch baking pan with parchment paper. Place cauliflower in prepared baking pan. Drizzle with the 2 tsp. oil and sprinkle with the ¼ tsp. salt; toss to coat. Roast about 20 minutes or until tender and browned. Remove from oven. Reduce oven temperature to 350°F.

2. Meanwhile, in a large saucepan cook macaroni according to package directions; drain. Rinse with cold water; drain again. Return macaroni to saucepan.

3. For cheese sauce, in a large nonstick skillet heat the 1 Tbsp. oil over medium heat. Add onion; cook about 3 minutes or until tender, stirring occasionally. Add garlic; cook and stir 30 seconds. In a bowl whisk together milk, flour, and the ½ tsp. salt until smooth; gradually stir into onion mixture. Cook and stir sauce until slightly thickened and bubbly. Reduce heat to low. Stir in cream cheese until melted. Remove from heat. Gradually add cheddar cheese, stirring just until melted.

4. Add cauliflower and cheese sauce to cooked macaroni; stir gently to combine. Transfer to a 3-qt. rectangular baking dish. In a bowl combine bread crumbs, Parmesan, and thyme. Drizzle with the 1 tsp. oil; toss to coat. Sprinkle crumb mixture over casserole. Bake, uncovered, 25 to 30 minutes or until heated through and crumbs are light brown.

NUMBER OF SERVINGS 8

PER SERVING *295 cal., 11 g fat (5 g sat. fat), 24 mg chol., 539 mg sodium, 36 g carb., 3 g fiber, 7 g sugars, 15 g pro.*

TORTELLINI-VEGETABLE BAKE

PREP 30 minutes **BAKE** 30 minutes at 350°F

- 2 9-oz. pkg. refrigerated cheese tortellini
- 1½ cups fresh sugar snap peas, trimmed and halved crosswise
- ½ cup thinly sliced carrot
- 1 Tbsp. butter
- 1 cup sliced fresh mushrooms
- ⅓ cup vegetable broth
- 2 tsp. all-purpose flour
- 1½ tsp. dried oregano, crushed
- ½ tsp. garlic salt
- ½ tsp. black pepper
- 1 cup milk
- 1 8-oz. pkg. cream cheese, cubed and softened
- 1 Tbsp. lemon juice
- 1 cup quartered cherry tomatoes
- ½ cup coarsely chopped red or green sweet pepper
- 2 Tbsp. grated Parmesan cheese

1. Preheat oven to 350°F. Cook tortellini according to package directions, adding sugar snap peas and carrot the last 1 minute of cooking; drain.

2. Meanwhile, in an extra-large skillet melt butter over medium heat. Add mushrooms; cook 5 minutes or until mushrooms are tender, stirring occasionally. Remove from skillet.

3. In a screw-top jar combine the next five ingredients (through black pepper). Cover and shake until smooth. Add to the same skillet. Add milk; cook and stir until thickened and bubbly. Add cream cheese; cook and stir until smooth. Remove from heat; stir in lemon juice. Stir tortellini mixture, mushrooms, tomatoes, and sweet pepper into cream cheese mixture. Spoon into an ungreased 3-qt. rectangular baking dish.

4. Bake, covered, 30 minutes or until heated through. Sprinkle with Parmesan cheese.

NUMBER OF SERVINGS 8

PER SERVING *347 cal., 17 g fat (9 g sat. fat), 60 mg chol., 528 mg sodium, 38 g carb., 3 g fiber, 7 g sugars, 13 g pro.*

 FLEX IT

Pack this pasta bake with lean protein. In Step 3, stir in 2 cups cubed cooked chicken or turkey breast with the tortellini mixture.

EASY PUMPKIN-ROASTED RED PEPPER MAC AND CHEESE

PREP 20 minutes **BAKE** 30 minutes at 375°F **STAND** 5 minutes

This veggie-base mac and cheese checks all the boxes for creamy comfort. Fontina cheese is a mild, melty cheese with a nutty taste. If you can't find it, substitute Swiss or provolone.

- 1 14.5-oz. pkg. dried multigrain rotini or penne pasta
- 1 15- to 16-oz. jar light Alfredo pasta sauce
- 1 15-oz. can pumpkin
- ½ cup chopped roasted red sweet peppers
- ½ cup water
- ¼ tsp. salt
- ⅛ tsp. black pepper
- 1½ cups shredded Fontina cheese (6 oz.)

1. Preheat oven to 375°F. Grease a 3-qt. rectangular baking dish.

2. In a large pot cook pasta according to package directions; drain. Return to pot. Stir in next the six ingredients (through black pepper). Stir in ½ cup of the cheese. Transfer to the prepared dish.

3. Bake, covered, 25 minutes. Sprinkle with the remaining 1 cup cheese. Bake, uncovered, 5 minutes more or until heated through and cheese is melted. Let stand 5 minutes before serving.

NUMBER OF SERVINGS 6

PER SERVING *446 cal., 15 g fat (9 g sat. fat), 62 mg chol., 800 mg sodium, 58 g carb., 7 g fiber, 7 g sugars, 21 g pro.*

**BARLEY-BUTTERNUT
CASSEROLE**
Recipe on page 106

GOOD GRAINS

QUINOA CAPRESE CASSEROLE

PREP 35 minutes **STAND** 5 minutes **BAKE** 30 minutes at 350°F

Turn flavors from classic caprese salad into a savory and satisfying hot dish. If you like, finish it like the salad and add a drizzle of balsamic glaze or a splash of balsamic vinegar.

Nonstick cooking spray

3 cups water

1½ cups quinoa, rinsed and drained

½ tsp. salt

2¼ cups marinara sauce

3 Tbsp. tomato paste

1 cup finely shredded Parmesan cheese

½ cup heavy cream

½ tsp. crushed red pepper

½ tsp. black pepper

2¼ cups grape tomatoes or cherry tomatoes, halved

1½ cups shredded part-skim mozzarella cheese (6 oz.)

1 cup shredded fresh basil

8 oz. fresh mozzarella, cut into ½-inch cubes

1. Preheat oven to 350°F. Lightly coat a 3-qt. rectangular baking dish with cooking spray. In a large saucepan combine the water, quinoa, and salt. Bring to boiling; reduce heat. Simmer, covered, 15 minutes or until water is absorbed. Let stand 5 minutes; uncover and fluff quinoa with a fork.

2. In a large saucepan combine marinara sauce and tomato paste. Stir over low heat until smooth. Stir in Parmesan cheese, cream, crushed red pepper, and black pepper. Bring to boiling; remove from heat. Gently stir in cooked quinoa. Using a rubber scraper, fold in 1½ cups of the grape tomatoes, the shredded mozzarella cheese, and ½ cup of the basil. Spread quinoa mixture into the prepared baking dish.

3. Top with the fresh mozzarella cheese. Bake, uncovered, 30 minutes or until heated. Top with the remaining grape tomatoes and basil.

NUMBER OF SERVINGS 6

PER SERVING *514 cal., 26 g fat (14 g sat. fat), 79 mg chol., 1,206 mg sodium, 41 g carb., 6 g fiber, 9 g sugars, 28 g pro.*

QUINOA-STUFFED SWEET PEPPERS

START TO FINISH 20 minutes

Classic stuffed peppers get a fresh, fast, and light update. Start with prepared frozen cooked quinoa as a base, and just add gooey cheese, crunchy seeds, and fresh herbs.

1 qt. water

2 medium red, green, orange, and/or yellow sweet peppers, halved lengthwise and seeded

1 12-oz. pkg. frozen cooked quinoa with vegetables

¾ cup shredded reduced-fat Mexican-style four-cheese blend (3 oz.)

5 Tbsp. salted dry-roasted sunflower seeds

2 Tbsp. snipped fresh basil or ½ tsp. dried basil, crushed

½ tsp. salt

1. Preheat broiler. In a medium saucepan bring the water to boiling. Add sweet pepper halves; boil 3 to 4 minutes or just until tender. Using tongs or a slotted spoon, transfer peppers to a foil-lined 13×9-inch baking pan.

2. Meanwhile, microwave the frozen quinoa according to package directions.

3. In a bowl stir together the hot cooked quinoa, ½ cup of the cheese, 4 Tbsp. of the sunflower seeds, the basil, and salt. Spoon quinoa mixture into pepper halves. Top with the remaining ¼ cup cheese.

4. Broil pepper halves 3 to 4 inches from the heat for 1 to 2 minutes or until the cheese is melted and starts to brown. Just before serving, sprinkle with the remaining 1 Tbsp. sunflower seeds.

NUMBER OF SERVINGS 4

PER SERVING *219 cal., 11 g fat (3 g sat. fat), 13 mg chol., 503 mg sodium, 22 g carb., 4 g fiber, 3 g sugars, 11 g pro.*

TOASTED BARLEY, MUSHROOM, AND ROASTED RED PEPPER ALFREDO

PREP 25 minutes   **COOK** 40 minutes   **BAKE** 50 minutes at 350°F

Nonstick cooking spray

½ cup butter

1½ cups regular pearled barley

1½ cups finely chopped onion

4 cloves garlic, minced

6 cups sliced fresh mushrooms

2½ cups vegetable broth

2 15-oz. jars light Alfredo pasta sauce

1 12-oz. jar roasted red sweet peppers, drained and coarsely chopped

2 cups frozen peas

2 tsp. dried Italian seasoning, crushed

2 cups torn sourdough bread slices

1. Preheat oven to 350°F. Coat a 3-qt. rectangular baking dish lightly with cooking spray. In an extra-large skillet melt ¼ cup of the butter over medium heat. Add barley; cook and stir 4 to 5 minutes or until barley is golden brown. Add onion and garlic; cook and stir 2 to 3 minutes or until onion is soft. Add mushrooms; cook and stir until mushrooms are tender. Carefully add broth. Bring to boiling; reduce heat. Simmer, covered, 40 to 45 minutes or until barley is tender and broth is absorbed.

2. Stir in Alfredo sauce, roasted red peppers, peas, and Italian seasoning. Spoon mixture into the prepared baking dish. Bake, covered, 20 minutes. Stir well. In a bowl microwave the remaining ¼ cup butter about 30 seconds or until melted. Brush melted butter on bread slices. Arrange slices over casserole. Bake, uncovered, 30 minutes or until hot and bubbly and bread is golden brown.

NUMBER OF SERVINGS 8

PER SERVING *423 cal., 18 g fat (13 g sat. fat), 75 mg chol., 1,135 mg sodium, 56 g carb., 9 g fiber, 9 g sugars, 12 g pro.*

FLEX IT

In Step 2, add 4-oz. smoked salmon, flaked, with skin and bones removed, with the Alfredo sauce. Serve with lemon wedges to squeeze over top.

BARLEY-BUTTERNUT CASSEROLE

PREP 35 minutes   **COOK** 45 minutes   **CHILL** 2 hours   **BAKE** 45 minutes at 350°F

7 to 8 slices maple-flavor bacon

1½ cups chopped onions

1 cup coarsely chopped celery

½ cup coarsely chopped red sweet pepper

4½ cups reduced-sodium chicken broth

½ cup dry white wine

1½ cups regular pearled barley

4 cups peeled butternut squash cut into ½-inch pieces

¼ cup snipped fresh sage

½ tsp. salt

½ tsp. black pepper

¼ cup reduced-sodium chicken broth (optional)

1. Lightly grease a 3-qt. rectangular baking dish. In a 4- to 5-qt. Dutch oven cook bacon over medium heat until crisp. Remove bacon and drain on paper towels, reserving 1 Tbsp. drippings in Dutch oven. Crumble bacon; set aside. Add onions, celery, and sweet pepper to the reserved drippings in Dutch oven. Cook over medium heat about 5 minutes or just until vegetables are tender, stirring occasionally.

2. Add the 4½ cups broth and the wine to Dutch oven; bring to boiling. Stir in barley. Return to boiling; reduce heat. Simmer, covered, 25 minutes. Stir in squash. Simmer, covered, about 20 minutes more or until squash and barley are tender, stirring occasionally. Remove from heat. Stir in crumbled bacon, snipped sage, salt, and black pepper. Transfer mixture to the prepared baking dish. Cover dish with foil. Chill 2 to 24 hours.

3. Preheat oven to 350°F. If desired, drizzle squash mixture with the ¼ cup broth to moisten, stirring gently to combine. Bake, covered, 45 to 55 minutes or until heated through, stirring once. If desired, garnish with additional fresh sage leaves.

NUMBER OF SERVINGS 10

PER SERVING *295 cal., 11 g fat (4 g sat. fat), 27 mg chol., 934 mg sodium, 34 g carb., 7 g fiber, 3 g sugars, 14 g pro.*

FLEX IT

This squash-studded casserole is easily made meatless by omitting the bacon and using vegetable broth instead of chicken broth. Substitute 1 Tbsp. olive oil for the bacon drippings.

SPICY SAUSAGE, MUSHROOM, AND POLENTA BAKE

PREP 50 minutes **BAKE** 1 hour at 350°F **STAND** 10 minutes

1 lb. bulk Italian sausage

1 medium fresh jalapeño chile pepper, seeded and finely chopped (tip, page 14) (optional)

2 cloves garlic, minced

1 24-oz. jar marinara sauce

1 Tbsp. olive oil

4 cups chopped fresh mushrooms

¾ cup thinly sliced green onions

2 cloves garlic, minced

1 tsp. snipped fresh rosemary

½ cup heavy cream

¼ cup dry white wine or chicken broth

½ tsp. salt

4 cups chicken broth

½ cup water

2 tsp. dried Italian seasoning, crushed

1½ cups cornmeal

2 cups shredded smoked provolone cheese (8 oz.)

1. Preheat oven to 350°F. In a large skillet cook sausage, jalapeño pepper, and 2 cloves garlic over medium-high heat until sausage is browned. Drain off fat. Stir in marinara sauce. Bring to boiling; reduce heat. Simmer, uncovered, 15 minutes, stirring frequently.

2. In another large skillet heat oil over medium heat. Add mushrooms, green onions, 2 cloves garlic, and rosemary. Cook about 5 minutes or until mushrooms are tender and liquid is evaporated, stirring occasionally. Stir in heavy cream, wine, and salt. Cook over low heat about 10 minutes or until mixture is thickened, stirring occasionally.

3. For polenta, in a large saucepan bring broth, the water, and Italian seasoning to boiling. Slowly add cornmeal, stirring constantly. Cook and stir until mixture returns to boiling; reduce heat to low. Cook 8 to 10 minutes or until thickened, stirring occasionally.

4. Preheat oven to 350°F. Meanwhile, grease a 3-qt. rectangular baking dish. Spread half the sausage mixture in the prepared dish. Working quickly, spread half the polenta over sausage mixture in dish. Top with mushroom mixture and half the cheese. Quickly spread the remaining polenta over top as evenly as possible. Top with the remaining sausage mixture and cheese.

5. Bake, uncovered, 1 to 1¼ hours or until heated through. Let stand 10 minutes before serving.

NUMBER OF SERVINGS 8

PER SERVING *495 cal., 30 g fat (14 g sat. fat), 83 mg chol., 1,504 mg sodium, 32 g carb., 3 g fiber, 7 g sugars, 21 g pro.*

PROSCIUTTO-STUFFED CHICKEN AND RICE BAKE

PREP 35 minutes **BAKE** 50 minutes at 375°F

If you can't find small chicken breast halves for this company-worthy casserole, purchase four large ones and cut them in half lengthwise.

- 8 5-oz. skinless, boneless chicken breast halves
- 8 thin slices prosciutto or 4 slices Canadian-style bacon, halved
- 2 8.8-oz. pouches cooked long grain white and wild rice
- 1 8.8-oz. pouch cooked white or brown rice
- ¼ cup butter, cut up
- 1 cup sliced green onions
- ¼ cup all-purpose flour
- ¼ tsp. black pepper
- 2 cups milk
- 1 cup coarsely chopped fresh asparagus or broccoli
- ¾ cup grated Parmesan cheese
- ¼ cup dry white wine, dry sherry, or milk
- ¾ cup panko bread crumbs
- ½ tsp. dried Italian seasoning, crushed

1. Preheat oven to 375°F. Lightly grease a 3-qt. rectangular baking dish. Using a small sharp knife, make a 2-inch-wide horizontal slit in the side of each chicken breast half to create a deep pocket. Stuff each pocket with a piece of the prosciutto, folding or cutting as necessary to fit.

2. In a bowl stir together rice from pouches; spread rice in the prepared baking dish. Top with chicken. Bake, covered, 25 minutes.

3. Meanwhile, for sauce, in a medium saucepan melt butter over medium heat. Add green onions; cook about 3 minutes or until tender, stirring frequently. Stir in flour and pepper until smooth. Add milk all at once. Cook and stir over medium-high heat until thickened and bubbly. Stir in asparagus, ½ cup of the cheese, and the wine. In a bowl combine the remaining ¼ cup cheese, the panko, and Italian seasoning.

4. Pour sauce over chicken; sprinkle with crumb mixture. Bake, uncovered, 25 to 30 minutes more or until chicken is done (165°F).

NUMBER OF SERVINGS 8

PER SERVING *512 cal., 18 g fat (6 g sat. fat), 117 mg chol., 802 mg sodium, 39 g carb., 2 g fiber, 5 g sugars, 43 g pro.*

FARRO, CHERRY TOMATO, AND CARROT GRATIN

PREP 20 minutes **COOK** 25 minutes **BAKE** 20 minutes at 400°F **STAND** 10 minutes

Regular unpearled farro is the whole grain that has the entire hull. It contains more nutrients but takes longer to cook. Pearled or semipearled farro is a good choice to save time.

Nonstick cooking spray

2 Tbsp. olive oil

½ cup chopped shallots

2 cups pearled farro or farro, rinsed and drained

1 32-oz. carton reduced-sodium chicken broth

½ tsp. salt

½ tsp. black pepper

1½ cups shredded carrots

1½ cups cherry tomatoes, halved

½ cup snipped fresh basil

6 eggs, lightly beaten

1½ cups half-and-half

¾ cup grated Asiago cheese (3 oz.)

½ cup soft whole wheat bread crumbs

3 Tbsp. coarsely snipped fresh Italian parsley

8 oz. fresh asparagus, trimmed

1. Lightly coat a 3-qt. rectangular baking dish with cooking spray. In a large saucepan heat oil over medium heat. Add shallots; reduce heat to medium-low. Cook 5 minutes or until tender. Add farro; stir to coat. Add broth, salt, and pepper. Return to boiling; reduce heat. Simmer, uncovered, 25 minutes for pearled farro (or 45 minutes for regular farro) or until tender. Remove from heat. Stir in carrots, tomatoes, and basil.

2. Preheat oven to 400°F. Spoon farro mixture into the prepared baking dish. In a bowl whisk together eggs, half-and-half, and cheese. Pour egg mixture over farro mixture; stir gently to combine. Spread evenly in dish.

3. In a bowl combine bread crumbs and parsley; sprinkle over farro mixture. Place asparagus spears in a crisscross pattern over top. Lightly coat asparagus and crumb mixture with cooking spray.

4. Bake, uncovered, 20 to 25 minutes or until a knife inserted near center comes out clean. Let stand 10 minutes before serving.

NUMBER OF SERVINGS 8

PER SERVING *396 cal., 17 g fat (7 g sat. fat), 165 mg chol., 604 mg sodium, 46 g carb., 7 g fiber, 6 g sugars, 18 g pro.*

SALMON VERACRUZ
Recipe on page 135

AROUND-THE-WORLD FLAVORS

GREEK CHICKEN AND PITA CASSEROLE

PREP 25 minutes **BAKE** 25 minutes at 400°F

4 cups chopped cooked chicken or turkey

3 medium zucchini, halved lengthwise and cut into ½-inch pieces (4 cups)

1 10.75-oz. can condensed cream of chicken soup

½ cup chopped red onion

½ cup chicken broth

1½ tsp. Greek seasoning*

2 cloves garlic, minced

2 6-inch pita bread rounds, cut into bite-size wedges

Nonstick cooking spray

1 cup chopped roma tomatoes

1 cup crumbled feta cheese (4 oz.)

½ cup pitted Kalamata olives, sliced

1. Preheat oven to 400°F. In a large bowl combine the first five ingredients (through broth), 1 tsp. of the Greek seasoning, and the garlic. Transfer mixture to an ungreased 3-qt. rectangular baking dish.

2. Coat pita wedges with cooking spray; sprinkle with the remaining ½ tsp. Greek seasoning. Place pita wedges on top of casserole. Bake, uncovered, 25 minutes or until heated through. Top with remaining ingredients.

NUMBER OF SERVINGS 6

*TIP If you can't find Greek seasoning in a store, make it at home. Combine 2 tsp. dried oregano, crushed; 1½ tsp. each onion powder and garlic powder; 1 tsp. each dried parsley flakes and black pepper; and ½ tsp. each ground cinnamon and ground nutmeg.

PER SERVING *407 cal., 19 g fat (7 g sat. fat), 109 mg chol., 1,185 mg sodium, 22 g carb., 2 g fiber, 5 g sugars, 35 g pro.*

Trim fat by using reduced-fat cream of chicken soup and reduced-fat feta cheese. Cut sodium with reduced-sodium chicken broth.

HONEY-CHILE CHICKEN ON COCONUT RICE

PREP 20 minutes **BAKE** 45 minutes at 350°F

Fresh lime juice is best, and with the need for only 1 tablespoon, it's easy to juice the fruit without a citrus reamer. Roll the whole lime on the countertop, cut it in half, insert a fork into the center, move the fork to break juice pockets, and squeeze.

Nonstick cooking spray

2 cups water

1 14-oz. can unsweetened light coconut milk

1¼ cups uncooked jasmine rice

½ tsp. salt

¾ cup chopped onion

¾ cup chopped yellow and/or red sweet pepper

2 tsp. olive oil

2 tsp. grated fresh ginger

2 cloves garlic, minced

1½ cups frozen peas

2 Tbsp. honey

2 Tbsp. Asian chili paste (sambal oelek)

1 Tbsp. lime juice

2 tsp. reduced-sodium soy sauce

3 cups chopped cooked chicken breast

Raw chip coconut, toasted (tip, page 21) (optional)

¼ cup snipped fresh cilantro

Lime wedges

1. Preheat oven to 350°F. Coat a 3-qt. rectangular baking dish with cooking spray. In a small saucepan bring the water and coconut milk to boiling; pour into prepared baking dish. Stir in rice and salt. Bake, covered, 30 minutes.

2. Meanwhile, in a large nonstick skillet cook onion and sweet pepper in hot oil over medium heat about 5 minutes or just until tender, stirring occasionally. Add ginger and garlic; cook and stir 1 minute more. Stir onion mixture and the peas into partially cooked rice.

3. In a medium bowl combine the next four ingredients (through soy sauce); stir in chicken. Spoon chicken mixture over rice mixture.

4. Bake, covered, 15 to 20 minutes more or until heated through and rice is tender. Sprinkle with coconut (if desired) and cilantro. Serve with lime wedges and/or additional chili paste.

NUMBER OF SERVINGS 8

PER SERVING *283 cal., 6 g fat (3 g sat. fat), 45 mg chol., 369 mg sodium, 36 g carb., 2 g fiber, 8 g sugars, 21 g pro.*

CHICKEN AND SPINACH PHYLLO BAKE

PREP 35 minutes **BAKE** 45 minutes at 375°F

Papery thin sheets of phyllo dough dry out quickly. Work with one sheet at a time, and keep the remaining phyllo covered with plastic wrap to prevent it from becoming dry and brittle.

Nonstick cooking spray

2 Tbsp. butter

2½ lb. uncooked ground chicken

1 cup chopped onion

3 10-oz. pkg. frozen chopped spinach, thawed and squeezed dry

1 tsp. black pepper

½ tsp. salt

½ tsp. ground nutmeg

¼ tsp. crushed red pepper

4 eggs, lightly beaten

1½ cups crumbled feta cheese (6 oz.)

1 Tbsp. snipped fresh oregano

16 sheets frozen phyllo dough (14×9-inch rectangles), thawed

1. Preheat oven to 375°F. Lightly coat a 3-qt. rectangular baking dish with cooking spray.

2. In an extra-large skillet melt butter over medium-high heat. Add ground chicken and onion; cook 8 minutes or until chicken is browned and onion is tender. Drain off fat. Stir in the next five ingredients (through crushed red pepper); cook and stir 5 minutes. Transfer mixture to a large bowl. Stir in eggs, cheese, and oregano.

3. Unfold phyllo dough. Using a sharp knife, cut a 1-inch strip off one short end of the phyllo stack; discard. Place a phyllo sheet in the prepared baking dish. Lightly coat phyllo sheet with cooking spray. Top with seven more sheets, coating each sheet with cooking spray. Spread chicken mixture over phyllo in dish. Top with the remaining eight phyllo sheets, coating each sheet with cooking spray and casually crumpling the top few sheets.

4. Bake, uncovered, 45 minutes or until heated through and phyllo is golden.

NUMBER OF SERVINGS 8

PER SERVING *530 cal., 29 g fat (13 g sat. fat), 273 mg chol., 1,024 mg sodium, 29 g carb., 4 g fiber, 4 g sugars, 41 g pro.*

CHICKEN CAESAR LASAGNA

PREP 35 minutes **BAKE** 50 minutes at 325°F **STAND** 15 minutes

Nonstick cooking spray

9 dried whole wheat or regular lasagna noodles

2 10-oz. containers refrigerated light or regular Alfredo pasta sauce

3 Tbsp. lemon juice

½ tsp. cracked black pepper

3 cups chopped cooked chicken breast

1 10-oz. pkg. frozen chopped spinach, thawed and squeezed dry

1 cup roasted red sweet peppers, chopped

¾ cup shredded Italian-blend cheeses (3 oz.)

Cherry or grape tomatoes, halved (optional)

1. Preheat oven to 325°F. Lightly coat a 3-qt. rectangular baking dish with cooking spray. Cook lasagna noodles according to package directions; Drain; rinse with cold water; drain again. Meanwhile, in a bowl stir together Alfredo sauce, lemon juice, and black pepper. Stir in chicken, spinach, and roasted sweet peppers.

2. Arrange three of the noodles in the prepared baking dish. Top with one-third of the chicken mixture. Repeat layers twice.

3. Bake, covered, 45 to 55 minutes or until heated. through Sprinkle with cheese. Bake, uncovered, 5 minutes more or until cheese is melted. Let stand 15 minutes before serving. If desired, top with tomatoes.

NUMBER OF SERVINGS 9

PER SERVING *268 cal., 10 g fat (6 g sat. fat), 68 mg chol., 557 mg sodium, 20 g carb., 2 g fiber, 3 g sugars, 24 g pro.*

CHICKEN AND TORTILLAS WITH TOMATILLO SAUCE

PREP 40 minutes **BAKE** 30 minutes at 350°F

Tomatillos, sometimes referred to as Mexican tomatoes, look like small green tomatoes that are covered with a papery skin. If you can't find fresh ones, use 5 cups quartered canned tomatillos, but do not cook in boiling water. Simply process as directed.

Nonstick cooking spray

1 lb. skinless, boneless chicken thighs

1 tsp. salt

2½ lb. fresh tomatillos, husked and quartered

2 fresh jalapeño chile peppers, seeded and cut up (tip, page 14)

3 cloves garlic, halved

2 cups shredded Mexican-style four-cheese blend (8 oz.)

4 oz. cream cheese, softened

1½ tsp. chili powder

8 8-inch flour tortillas

Cherry tomatoes, halved and/or quartered (optional)

Fresh cilantro sprigs (optional)

1. Preheat oven to 350°F. Coat a 3-qt. rectangular baking dish with cooking spray. In a large saucepan combine chicken and enough cold water to cover; add ½ tsp. of the salt. Bring to boiling; reduce heat. Simmer, covered, 15 minutes or until chicken is tender. Using a slotted spoon, transfer chicken to a large bowl; discard cooking liquid. When chicken is cool enough to handle, shred using two forks.

2. Meanwhile, bring a large pot of water to boiling. Add tomatillos and cook 3 minutes; drain. Transfer tomatillos to a food processor or blender; add jalapeño peppers, garlic, and the remaining ½ tsp. salt. Cover and process until smooth. In a bowl stir together shredded cheese, cream cheese, and chili powder.

3. Spread one-third of the tomatillo mixture in the prepared baking dish. Top with two of the tortillas, half the chicken, and half the cheese mixture. Top with another two tortillas, another one-third of the tomatillo mixture, and another two tortillas. Top with remaining chicken, cheese mixture, tortillas, and tomatillo mixture.

4. Bake, covered, 30 minutes or until bubbly around the edges. If desired, top with cherry tomatoes and cilantro.

NUMBER OF SERVINGS 8

PER SERVING *422 cal., 21 g fat (9 g sat. fat), 94 mg chol., 1,094 mg sodium, 36 g carb., 3 g fiber, 6 g sugars, 24 g pro.*

INDIAN-SPICED CHICKEN CASSEROLE

PREP 50 minutes **BAKE** 1 hour 10 minutes at 350°F

- 8 oz. dried vermicelli
- 3 Tbsp. butter
- ½ cup finely chopped onion
- 1 Tbsp. lemon juice
- 1 Tbsp. ginger-garlic paste
- 2 tsp. garam masala
- 2 tsp. ground cumin
- 2 tsp. chili powder
- 1 cup tomato puree
- 1 6-oz. carton plain yogurt
- ¾ cup heavy cream
- ¼ tsp. salt
- ¼ tsp. cayenne pepper
- 3 6-oz. pkg. refrigerated grilled chicken breast strips, chopped
- 1 lb. paneer, cut into ½-inch cubes; crumbled queso fresco; or shredded farmer cheese
- 2 8-oz. pkg. cream cheese, softened
- 1 tsp. garam masala
- 1 tsp. ground cumin
- 1 tsp. ground turmeric
- 2 10-oz. pkg. frozen chopped spinach, thawed and well drained
  Fresh Italian parsley leaves (optional)

1. Preheat oven to 350°F. Cook vermicelli according to package directions; drain. Rinse with cold water; drain again.

2. Meanwhile, in a large skillet melt butter over medium-high heat. Add onion; cook about 4 minutes or until onion is tender, stirring occasionally. Add the next five ingredients (through chili powder); cook and stir 1 minute. Carefully add tomato puree; cook and stir 2 minutes more. Stir in yogurt, cream, salt, and cayenne pepper. Stir in chicken. Cook, uncovered, over low heat 10 minutes, stirring frequently.

3. In a large bowl combine three-fourths of the paneer and the next four ingredients (through turmeric). Stir in spinach.

4. Butter a 3-qt. rectangular baking dish. Transfer half the chicken mixture to the prepared dish. Top with half the vermicelli; spread the spinach mixture over vermicelli. Top with remaining vermicelli and remaining chicken mixture.

5. Bake, covered, 65 to 70 minutes or until heated through. Sprinkle with the remaining paneer. Bake, uncovered, 5 minutes. If desired, sprinkle with parsley.

NUMBER OF SERVINGS 12

PER SERVING *428 cal., 27 g fat (15 g sat. fat), 111 mg chol., 779 mg sodium, 25 g carb., 3 g fiber, 5 g sugars, 22 g pro.*

Two packages of cream cheese is a hefty amount—you can cut the fat substantially by using the reduced-fat version.

ITALIAN ORZO BAKE WITH TURKEY MEATBALLS

PREP 40 minutes **BAKE** 25 minutes at 400°F

Nonstick cooking spray

4 cups reduced-sodium chicken broth

16 oz. dried orzo pasta

6 oz. thinly sliced pancetta, chopped, or 6 slices bacon, chopped

1 cup chopped onion

2 cloves garlic, minced

1 cup dry white wine or reduced-sodium chicken broth

1 cup shredded provolone cheese (4 oz.)

½ cup chopped roasted red sweet peppers

½ cup heavy cream

¼ tsp. salt

¼ tsp. black pepper

1 12-oz. pkg. refrigerated cooked Italian turkey meatballs (12)

½ cup panko bread crumbs

⅓ cup finely shredded Parmesan cheese

1 tsp. dried thyme, crushed

2 Tbsp. olive oil

Snipped fresh Italian parsley (optional)

1. Preheat oven to 400°F. Lightly coat a 3-qt. rectangular baking dish with cooking spray.

2. In a 4-qt. Dutch oven bring broth to boiling. Stir in orzo. Cook, uncovered, 6 to 7 minutes or until orzo is almost tender and liquid is absorbed, stirring occasionally. Remove from heat.

3. In a large skillet cook and stir pancetta over medium heat until browned and crisp. Remove pancetta; drain on paper towels. Reserve 1 Tbsp. drippings in skillet. Cook onion in reserved drippings over medium heat 3 to 4 minutes or until tender, stirring occasionally. Add garlic; cook and stir 1 minute. Remove from heat. Add wine, stirring to scrape up any browned bits in pan. Return to heat; simmer, uncovered, about 5 minutes or until wine is reduced by half. Add wine mixture to orzo in Dutch oven. Stir in pancetta and the next five ingredients (through black pepper). Transfer to the prepared baking dish.

4. Add meatballs, pressing lightly into orzo mixture. In a bowl stir together panko, Parmesan cheese, and thyme. Drizzle with oil; toss to coat. Sprinkle over meatballs and orzo mixture.

5. Bake, uncovered, 25 minutes or until bubbly and crumbs are golden. If desired, sprinkle with parsley.

NUMBER OF SERVINGS 6

PER SERVING *743 cal., 32 g fat (12 g sat. fat), 81 mg chol., 1,211 mg sodium, 72 g carb., 3 g fiber, 5 g sugars, 35 g pro.*

MEXICAN CHILES EN NOGADA

PREP 30 minutes **BAKE** 15 minutes at 425°F + 20 minutes at 350°F **STAND** 15 minutes

8 large fresh poblano chile peppers

12 oz. ground pork

½ cup chopped onion

1 medium fresh jalapeño chile pepper, seeded and finely chopped (tip, page 14) (optional)

1 clove garlic, minced

Vegetable oil (optional)

1⅓ cups chopped peeled and seeded tomatoes

1 cup coarsely shredded unpeeled pear

1 8.75-oz. can whole kernel corn, drained

¼ cup raisins

½ tsp. salt

¼ tsp. ground cinnamon

¼ tsp. black pepper

½ cup pecans or pine nuts, toasted (tip, page 21)

1 8-oz. carton sour cream

2 Tbsp. milk

1 tsp. lime juice

⅛ tsp. ground cinnamon

Chili powder (optional)

Pumpkin seeds (pepitas), toasted (tip, page 21)

1. Preheat oven to 425°F. Place whole poblano peppers on a foil-lined baking sheet. Roast 15 to 20 minutes or until peppers are charred and tender, turning once or twice. Bring foil up around peppers and fold edges together to enclose. Let stand 15 minutes or until cool enough to handle. Using a sharp knife, gently remove skins from peppers (tip, page 14). Carefully cut one vertical slit the length of each pepper, keeping stem intact. Remove seeds. Reduce oven temperature to 350°F.

2. Meanwhile, for filling, in a large skillet cook pork, onion, jalapeño pepper, and garlic over medium heat until pork is browned, adding oil if necessary to prevent sticking. Drain off any fat. Stir in the next seven ingredients (through black pepper). Simmer, uncovered, 10 minutes. Cool.

3. Spoon about ½ cup of the filling into each poblano pepper. Place stuffed peppers in an ungreased 3-qt. rectangular baking dish. Bake, uncovered, 20 minutes or until heated through.

4. For sauce, place nuts in a blender or food processor. Cover and blend or process until finely ground. In a bowl stir together ground nuts and the next four ingredients (through cinnamon). Spoon sauce over stuffed peppers. Sprinkle with chili powder (if desired) and pumpkin seeds.

NUMBER OF SERVINGS 8

PER SERVING *290 cal., 18 g fat (6 g sat. fat), 46 mg chol., 235 mg sodium, 23 g carb., 3 g fiber, 8 g sugars, 12 g pro.*

Prepare as directed through Step 3, except do not bake. Cover and refrigerate up to 8 hours. Uncover and continue as directed, baking 30 minutes or until heated through.

FRENCH CHOUCROUTE GARNI

PREP 45 minutes   **COOL** 10 minutes   **BAKE** 45 minutes at 350°F

- 1 Tbsp. olive oil or vegetable oil
- 1 medium red onion, cut into thin wedges
- 4 cloves garlic, minced
- 1 12-oz. bottle ale or beer
- 1½ cups apple juice, apple cider, or chicken broth
- 3 Tbsp. cornstarch
- 3 Tbsp. coarse-ground brown mustard
- 1 Tbsp. caraway seeds
- 1 Tbsp. snipped fresh rosemary
- ½ tsp. cracked black pepper
- 12 oz. fingerling potatoes and/or tiny new potatoes, quartered
- 1½ cups sliced carrots
- 2 7.5-oz. pkg. smoked boneless pork chops, cut into bite-size pieces, or two 6-oz. pkg. Canadian-style bacon, cut into chunks
- 1 lb. smoked kielbasa, halved lengthwise and bias-sliced into 1-inch pieces
- 2 medium cooking apples, such as Granny Smith or Jonagold, cored and cut into chunks
- 1 14.5-oz. can sauerkraut, rinsed, drained, and squeezed dry

1. In a medium saucepan heat oil over medium heat. Add onion and garlic; cook about 4 minutes or until tender, stirring occasionally. Add ale. In a bowl stir together the next six ingredients (through pepper); stir into ale mixture. Cook and stir until thickened and bubbly. Cool 10 minutes.

2. Meanwhile, in a large saucepan cook potatoes and carrots, covered, in enough boiling lightly salted water to cover about 10 minutes or until slightly tender but still firm. Drain.

3. Preheat oven to 350°F. In an ungreased 3-qt. rectangular baking dish layer pork chop pieces, kielbasa pieces, potato mixture, apples, and sauerkraut. Pour ale mixture over layers in baking dish.

4. Bake, covered, 45 to 60 minutes or until potatoes are tender and center is heated. If desired, serve with additional coarse-ground brown mustard.

NUMBER OF SERVINGS 12

PER SERVING *289 cal., 15 g fat (5 g sat. fat), 49 mg chol., 1,039 mg sodium, 23 g carb., 3 g fiber, 9 g sugars, 14 g pro.*

SWEET POTATO-CHORIZO LASAGNA

PREP 30 minutes **BAKE** 1 hour 45 minutes at 375°F **STAND** 20 minutes

No-boil lasagna noodles may seem like an easy shortcut, but do not use them when making this creamy version. Because the homemade sweet potato sauce is thicker than a traditional tomato sauce, there's not enough moisture in the dish to cook the noodles.

4 medium sweet potatoes (about 2 lb.)

1¼ cups milk

2 Tbsp. lime juice

2 tsp. ground cumin

3 7.5-oz. links uncooked chorizo sausage

12 dried lasagna noodles

Olive oil

¼ cup thinly sliced green onions

¼ cup chopped fresh cilantro

1½ cups shredded sharp white cheddar cheese (6 oz.)

1. Preheat oven to 375°F. For sweet potato sauce, place sweet potatoes on a foil-lined baking sheet. Bake about 60 minutes or until tender when pierced with a fork. Remove from oven; cool. Peel; discard skin. Transfer sweet potatoes to a food processor. Add milk, lime juice, and cumin. Cover; process until smooth.

2. In a large skillet cook chorizo over medium heat about 5 minutes or until done (160°F). Remove from heat. Drain off fat.

3. Meanwhile, cook noodles according to package directions until tender but still firm (al dente). Drain; rinse with cold water. Drain well.

4. Drizzle bottom of a 3-qt. rectangular baking dish with olive oil. Arrange 3 noodles in a single layer over oil. Spread one-fourth of sweet potato sauce over noodles. Top with one-fourth each of the chorizo, green onions, cilantro, and cheddar cheese. Repeat layers three more times. Cover with a piece of parchment brushed with olive oil, coated side down; seal tightly with foil.

5. Bake 40 minutes. Uncover; bake 5 minutes more or until cheese is golden brown and lasagna is bubbly. Let stand 20 minutes before serving.

NUMBER OF SERVINGS 8

PER SERVING *684 cal., 41 g fat (17 g sat. fat), 96 mg chol., 1,184 mg sodium, 46 g carb., 4 g fiber, 7 g sugars, 32 g pro.*

SALMON VERACRUZ

PREP 30 minutes **BAKE** 20 minutes at 350°F

1½ lb. fresh or frozen skinless salmon fillet, about ¾ inch thick

1 Tbsp. butter

1 Tbsp. olive oil

1½ cups dried orzo pasta (9 oz.)

3 cups vegetable broth or reduced-sodium chicken broth

¼ cup pimiento-stuffed green olives, sliced

2 cups chopped tomatoes

1 fresh jalapeño chile pepper, seeded and finely chopped (tip, page 14)

2 Tbsp. lime juice

1 Tbsp. capers, drained

½ tsp. sugar

1. Thaw salmon, if frozen. Preheat oven to 350°F. Rinse salmon; pat dry. If necessary, cut into six portions.

2. In a large skillet heat butter and oil over medium-high heat. Add orzo; cook and stir 5 minutes or until golden. Remove from heat; stir in broth. Return to heat. Simmer, uncovered, about 8 minutes or just until orzo is tender and most of the liquid is absorbed. Stir in 2 Tbsp. of the olives. Transfer to a 3-qt. rectangular baking dish. Top with salmon.

3. Bake, covered, 20 to 25 minutes or until salmon flakes easily.

4. Meanwhile, in a bowl combine the remaining 2 Tbsp. olives and the remaining ingredients. Spoon over salmon mixture.

NUMBER OF SERVINGS 6

PER SERVING *386 cal., 13 g fat (3 g sat. fat), 67 mg chol., 465 mg sodium, 37 g carb., 2 g fiber, 4 g sugars, 29 g pro.*

BAKED CAJUN SEAFOOD AND RICE

PREP 50 minutes **BAKE** 25 minutes at 350°F

Refrigerated pasteurized lump crabmeat is an excellent alternative to traditional canned crabmeat or more expensive fresh crab. Look for it at the meat and seafood counter of your supermarket.

1 lb. fresh or frozen peeled and deveined small shrimp

1 Tbsp. butter

¾ cup chopped green sweet pepper

½ cup chopped onion

½ cup sliced celery

2 cloves garlic, minced

½ tsp. dried thyme, crushed

3 cups cooked long grain white rice

4 slices bacon, chopped

8 cups torn, stemmed fresh kale or spinach

2 Tbsp. butter

2 Tbsp. all-purpose flour

1½ tsp. Cajun seasoning

2 cups milk

2 cups shredded Monterey Jack cheese (8 oz.)

12 oz. cooked crabmeat, flaked

½ cup shredded Parmesan cheese (2 oz.)

½ cup chopped green onions

1. Thaw shrimp, if frozen. Rinse shrimp; pat dry. Preheat oven to 350°F. In a large skillet melt the 1 Tbsp. butter over medium heat. Add sweet pepper, onion, celery, and garlic; cook 4 minutes or until vegetables are tender, stirring occasionally. Add thyme; cook and stir 1 minute more. Transfer mixture to a bowl. Stir in cooked rice.

2. In the same skillet cook bacon over medium heat until crisp. Add kale; cook and stir 3 to 5 minutes or until wilted and tender. Remove from heat.

3. For sauce, in a small saucepan melt the 2 Tbsp. butter over medium heat. Stir in flour and Cajun seasoning; cook and stir 1 minute. Gradually stir in milk. Cook and stir until thickened and bubbly. Cook and stir 1 minute more. Reduce heat to low. Gradually add Monterey Jack cheese, stirring until cheese is melted.

4. Lightly grease a 3-qt. rectangular baking dish. Spread half the rice mixture in the prepared baking dish. Top with half the kale mixture, half the shrimp, half the crabmeat, and half the sauce. Repeat layers. Sprinkle with Parmesan cheese.

5. Bake, uncovered, 25 to 30 minutes or until bubbly. Sprinkle with green onions.

NUMBER OF SERVINGS 8

PER SERVING *440 cal., 19 g fat (11 g sat. fat), 158 mg chol., 986 mg sodium, 30 g carb., 3 g fiber, 6 g sugars, 36 g pro.*

ZA'ATAR RICE-STUFFED PEPPERS

PREP 30 minutes **BAKE** 30 minutes at 400°F

Za'atar is an herb and spice blend widely used in Arabic cooking that is made up of dried oregano, thyme, and savory as well as salt, sesame seeds, and dried sumac, which has a fruity, astringent flavor. Look for it at specialty spice stores, Middle Eastern markets, or online.

1 Tbsp. olive oil

¾ cup chopped onion

1 Tbsp. za'atar spice mix

2 cloves garlic, minced

¼ tsp. crushed red pepper

⅛ tsp. salt

⅛ tsp. black pepper

1 15-oz. can garbanzo beans (chickpeas), rinsed and drained

1 15-oz. can tomato puree

3 cups cooked basmati rice

4 yellow, red, and/or green sweet peppers

½ cup water

1 5.3-oz. carton plain fat-free Greek yogurt

Chopped cucumber and/or snipped fresh Italian parsley (optional)

Lemon wedges (optional)

1. Preheat oven to 400°F. In a large skillet heat oil over medium heat. Add onion; cook 5 minutes or until tender, stirring occasionally. Add the next five ingredients (through black pepper); cook and stir 1 minute more. Stir in beans and tomato puree; heat. Stir in rice.

2. Halve sweet peppers lengthwise; remove and discard seeds and membranes. Fill pepper halves with rice mixture. Place stuffed peppers in a 3-qt. rectangular baking dish. Pour the water into dish around stuffed peppers.

3. Bake, covered, about 30 minutes or until peppers are crisp-tender. Top with yogurt and, if desired, cucumber, parsley, and/or additional za'atar spice mix. If desired, serve with lemon wedges.

NUMBER OF SERVINGS 8

PER SERVING *192 cal., 3 g fat (0g sat. fat), 0 mg chol., 331 mg sodium, 36 g carb., 4 g fiber, 6 g sugars, 8 g pro.*

Bulk up these tasty peppers with lean protein. Stir in 1½ cups chopped cooked chicken breast with the rice.

MAKE AHEAD

Stuff peppers as directed, but do not add water. Cover with foil and refrigerate up to 24 hours. Add water and bake as directed.

MAKE-IT-MINE
ONE-PAN DINNER
Recipe on page 146

ONE-PAN DINNERS

MINI MEAT LOAVES WITH POTATOES AND BEANS

PREP 30 minutes **BAKE** 40 minutes at 350°F

1 egg, lightly beaten

3 Tbsp. fine dry bread crumbs

¼ cup shredded carrot

¼ cup finely chopped onion

1 Tbsp. ketchup

1 tsp. yellow mustard

1 tsp. Worcestershire sauce

1 clove garlic, minced

1 lb. extra-lean ground beef

¼ cup ketchup

2 Tbsp. packed brown sugar

1 tsp. yellow mustard

8 oz. fingerling potatoes

2 tsp. olive oil

1 tsp. dried thyme

¼ tsp. salt

¼ tsp. black pepper

8 oz. fresh green beans, trimmed

1. Preheat oven to 350°F. Line a 13×9-inch baking pan with foil. In a bowl stir together the first eight ingredients (through garlic). Add beef; mix well. Divide into four equal portions and shape into round loaves. Arrange in one half of the pan. In a bowl stir together the ¼ cup ketchup, the brown sugar, and 1 tsp. mustard. Spread over meat loaves.

2. In another bowl combine the next five ingredients (through pepper); toss to coat. Arrange in the opposite half of pan.

3. Bake, uncovered, 40 to 45 minutes or until meat loaves are done (160°F) and vegetables are tender, adding green beans to the potato mixture after 20 minutes.

NUMBER OF SERVINGS 4

PER SERVING *345 cal., 12 g fat (4 g sat. fat), 118 mg chol., 512 mg sodium, 31 g carb., 4 g fiber, 15 g sugars, 29 g pro.*

PORK CHOPS WITH ROASTED VEGETABLES AND BALSAMIC DRIZZLE

PREP 25 minutes   **ROAST** 35 minutes at 425°F

Get smokehouse flavor indoors! Smoked black pepper has been infused with smoke flavor to add depth and dimension to recipes.

¼ cup balsamic vinegar

1 Tbsp. tomato paste

1 Tbsp. honey

¾ tsp. smoked black pepper or black pepper

½ tsp. salt

1 large sweet potato (12 oz.), cut into ½-inch wedges

8 oz. fresh Brussels sprouts, trimmed and halved (2 cups)

1 medium parsnip, cut into ½-inch slices (1 cup)

3 Tbsp. olive oil

4 4- to 5-oz. boneless pork loin chops, cut 1 inch thick and trimmed

1 tsp. dried herbes de Provence

½ cup crumbled goat cheese (chèvre) (2 oz.)

1. Preheat oven to 425°F. In a bowl combine vinegar, tomato paste, honey, and ¼ tsp. each of the pepper and salt.

2. In a 3-qt. rectangular baking dish combine sweet potato, Brussels sprouts, and parsnip. Drizzle with 2 Tbsp. of the oil; toss to coat. Roast, uncovered, 25 minutes.

3. Meanwhile, sprinkle chops with herbes de Provence and the remaining ½ tsp. pepper and ¼ tsp. salt. In a large skillet heat the remaining 1 Tbsp. oil over medium-high heat. Add chops; cook 2 minutes or until browned, turning once.

4. Place chops on top of vegetables. Roast 10 to 15 minutes more or until chops are done (145°F) and vegetables are tender. Sprinkle with cheese. Drizzle with balsamic mixture.

NUMBER OF SERVINGS 4

PER SERVING *442 cal., 19 g fat (6 g sat. fat), 89 mg chol., 516 mg sodium, 36 g carb., 7 g fiber, 14 g sugars, 32 g pro.*

MAKE-IT-MINE ONE-PAN DINNER

PREP 15 minutes **ROAST** 25 minutes at 425°F **STAND** 3 minutes

Master this easy cooking method to vary meals every week. The versatility of pork tenderloin and chicken breast invite creativity. Choose a rub, then add whatever seasonal vegetables are best. Finish the dish with a flavorful sauce, dressing, or squeeze of citrus.

BASE RECIPE

- 1 tsp. olive oil
- 1 1-lb. natural pork tenderloin or two 8-oz. skinless boneless chicken breast halves
- 1 recipe Rub
- 4 cups Vegetables
- 1 Tbsp. olive oil
- ½ tsp. salt
- ½ tsp. black pepper
  Finishes (optional)

1. Preheat oven to 425°F. Lightly brush the 1 tsp. olive oil over pork. Using your fingers, evenly spread Rub over pork. Place pork in a 13×9-inch baking pan. (For easy cleanup, line pan with foil.)

2. Place Vegetables in a bowl. Drizzle with the 1 Tbsp. olive oil and sprinkle with salt and black pepper. Arrange vegetables around pork in pan.

3. Roast, uncovered, 25 to 30 minutes or until vegetables are tender and pork is done (145°F) (for chicken, roast 20 to 25 minutes or until done [165°F]). Cover pork with foil; let stand 3 minutes. Slice pork and serve with vegetables, and, if desired, Finishes.

NUMBER OF SERVINGS 4

PICK A RUB

- ✱ **Greek** 2 tsp. dried oregano, crushed; 1 tsp. dried basil, crushed; ½ tsp. lemon-pepper seasoning; and ¼ tsp. garlic powder.

- ✱ **BBQ** 1 Tbsp. packed brown sugar, 2 tsp. chili powder, ½ tsp. smoked paprika, and ¼ tsp. salt

- ✱ **Mustard-Thyme** 1 Tbsp. yellow mustard; 1 Tbsp. honey; ½ tsp. dried thyme; crushed; and ¼ tsp. black pepper

- ✱ **Sweet 'n' Spicy** 1 Tbsp. packed brown sugar, ½ tsp. pumpkin pie spice, ½ tsp. orange zest, ¼ tsp. salt, and ⅛ to ¼ tsp. cayenne pepper

PICK VEGETABLES

- ✱ 1-inch cubes potatoes, peeled sweet potatoes, fingerlings, and/or whole tiny new potatoes

- ✱ 1-inch cubes peeled butternut or acorn squash, ½-inch slices delicata squash, and/or 1-inch cubes summer squash

- ✱ Sliced carrots and/or parsnips

- ✱ ½-inch wedges red and/or yellow onion

- ✱ ½-inch wedges fennel bulb

- ✱ Brussels sprouts (halved, if large)

- ✱ Cauliflower florets

- ✱ Whole cherry and/or grape tomatoes

- ✱ 1-inch pieces sweet peppers

- ✱ Button and/or cremini mushrooms, halved

- ✱ Whole garlic cloves

PICK A FINISH

- ✱ Basil pesto
- ✱ Lemon, lime, or orange wedges
- ✱ Barbecue sauce
- ✱ Plain Greek yogurt or tzatziki sauce
- ✱ Light vinaigrette dressing

MEDITERRANEAN SAUSAGE AND GRAPES

PREP 30 minutes **BAKE** 50 minutes at 350°F

1½ lb. whole seedless red grapes

1 16-oz. tube refrigerated cooked polenta, cut into ½-inch pieces

1 small red onion, cut into thin wedges

1 tsp. snipped fresh rosemary

1 to 2 Tbsp. olive oil

6 uncooked sweet and/or spicy Italian sausage links (about 1½ lb. total)

1 to 2 Tbsp. balsamic vinegar

1. Preheat oven to 350°F. In an ungreased 3-qt. rectangular baking dish combine grapes, polenta, onion, and rosemary. Drizzle with oil; toss gently to coat.

2. Using a fork, prick each sausage in several places. Add sausages to baking dish, pressing lightly into grape mixture.

3. Bake, uncovered, 50 to 60 minutes or until sausages are cooked through and grapes are slightly shriveled. Drizzle with vinegar; toss gently to coat.

NUMBER OF SERVINGS 4

PER SERVING *478 cal., 20 g fat (8 g sat. fat), 58 mg chol., 1,156 mg sodium, 46 g carb., 2 g fiber, 30 g sugars, 31 g pro.*

Look for uncooked turkey or chicken Italian sausage links to substitute for pork sausage varieties to cut some of the fat.

LEMON CHICKEN AND POTATOES

PREP 20 minutes **ROAST** 30 minutes at 450°F

Roasting lemons with the potatoes and chicken does a couple things. Oils in the skin are released to infuse the chicken and potatoes with flavor, while the acidity of the juice mellows, for an excellent main ingredient to make a simple dressing.

4 bone-in chicken breast halves (about 1½ lb. total)

1 lb. fingerling or baby Yukon gold potatoes

3 lemons, halved crosswise

⅓ cup pitted green and/or black olives

6 Tbsp. olive oil

Salt and black pepper

1 Tbsp. honey

6 cups arugula and/or mixed salad greens

1. Preheat oven to 450°F. Place chicken, potatoes, lemons, and olives in an ungreased 3-qt. rectangular baking dish. Drizzle with 2 Tbsp. of the olive oil; toss to coat. Spread mixture in a single layer in baking dish, arranging chicken skin sides up and lemons cut sides up. Sprinkle with salt and pepper.

2. Roast, uncovered, about 30 minutes or until chicken is done (170°F), potatoes are tender, and lemons are brown on the edges and soft throughout. Remove from oven. Remove lemons from dish; cover chicken, potatoes, and olives with foil to keep warm.

3. When lemons are cool enough to handle, squeeze juice and pulp into a small bowl; discard any seeds. Whisk in the remaining 4 Tbsp. olive oil and the honey. Season to taste with salt and pepper.

4. Serve chicken, potatoes, and olives over arugula. Drizzle with lemon dressing; sprinkle with additional pepper.

NUMBER OF SERVINGS 4

PER SERVING *573 cal., 40 g fat (8 g sat. fat), 87 mg chol., 435 mg sodium, 34 g carb., 7 g fiber, 8 g sugars, 26 g pro.*

HERB-ROASTED CHICKEN AND VEGETABLES

PREP 30 minutes **ROAST** 1 hour 15 minutes at 375°F **STAND** 10 minutes

1 3½- to 4-lb. whole broiler chicken

4 Tbsp. butter, melted

2 cloves garlic, minced

1 tsp. dried basil, crushed

1 tsp. dried sage, crushed

½ tsp. dried thyme, crushed

½ tsp. salt

½ tsp. black pepper

1 lb. red potatoes, cut into 1-inch pieces

6 medium carrots, halved lengthwise and cut into 1-inch pieces

1 medium turnip, peeled and cut into 1½-inch pieces

1 medium onion, cut into 1-inch chunks

1 Tbsp. vegetable oil

1. Preheat oven to 375°F. Rinse chicken body cavity; pat dry with paper towels. Skewer neck skin to back; tie legs to tail. Twist wing tips under back. Place chicken, breast side up, on a rack in a shallow roasting pan. Brush with 2 Tbsp. of the melted butter; rub with garlic.

2. In a bowl stir together basil, sage, thyme, and ¼ tsp. each of the salt and pepper; rub onto chicken. Insert a meat thermometer into center of an inside thigh muscle. (Thermometer should not touch bone.)

3. In a large bowl combine potatoes, carrots, turnip, and onion. Add the remaining 2 Tbsp. melted butter, the oil, and the remaining ¼ tsp. each salt and pepper; toss to coat vegetables. Arrange vegetables around chicken in pan.

4. Roast, uncovered, 75 to 90 minutes or until drumsticks move easily in sockets and chicken is no longer pink (at least 170°F), stirring vegetables once or twice. Remove chicken from oven. Cover; let stand 10 minutes before carving.

NUMBER OF SERVINGS 4

PER SERVING *590 cal., 39 g fat (14 g sat. fat), 201 mg chol., 558 mg sodium, 27 g carb., 4 g fiber, 5 g sugars, 35 g pro.*

ITALIAN ROASTED CHICKEN AND VEGETABLE TOSS

PREP 25 minutes   **ROAST** 50 minutes at 375°F

Use economical bone-in chicken breast for this recipe. Leaving the skin on and bone in keeps the meat moist and creates pan juices, which are essential for the final dish.

Nonstick cooking spray

2 bone-in chicken breast halves (about 2 lb. total)

½ cup peeled fresh baby carrots

1 medium onion, cut into 8 wedges (½ cup)

1 small zucchini, cut into 1-inch chunks (about 1 cup)

1 cup fresh mushrooms, halved

1 medium red or green sweet pepper, cut into 1-inch chunks (about ¾ cup)

3 Tbsp. olive oil

¼ tsp. salt

¼ tsp. black pepper

2 Tbsp. balsamic vinegar

1 tsp. dried Italian seasoning, crushed

8 cups mixed salad greens

¼ cup shredded Parmesan cheese (1 oz.)

1. Preheat oven to 375°F. Coat a 13×9-inch baking pan with cooking spray or line with foil. Arrange chicken, skin sides up, in half the roasting pan. In the opposite half arrange carrots and onion wedges. Roast, uncovered, 25 minutes.

2. Remove pan from oven. Add zucchini, mushrooms, and sweet pepper to the carrots and onion (dish will be full). Drizzle chicken and vegetables with 2 Tbsp. of the olive oil and sprinkle with the salt and black pepper.

3. Roast, uncovered, 25 minutes more or until chicken is done (170°F) and vegetables are tender. Set chicken aside until cool enough to handle. Transfer vegetables to a bowl.

4. Remove and discard chicken skin and bones. Shred chicken using two forks. Add chicken and any juices in pan to vegetables (if desired, skim fat from juices); toss to coat. In a bowl whisk together vinegar, the remaining 1 Tbsp. olive oil, and the Italian seasoning. Add to chicken and vegetables; toss to coat.

5. Arrange salad greens on a platter or divide among six plates. Spoon chicken and vegetables over greens. Sprinkle with cheese.

NUMBER OF SERVINGS 6

PER SERVING *249 cal., 14 g fat (3 g sat. fat), 70 mg chol., 235 mg sodium, 6 g carb., 2 g fiber, 4 g sugars, 25 g pro.*

ROASTED CURRIED CHICKEN AND CAULIFLOWER

PREP 20 minutes **ROAST** 50 minutes at 375°F

¼ cup honey*

¼ cup Dijon-style mustard*

2 Tbsp. olive oil

1 Tbsp. curry powder

3 cloves garlic, minced

¼ tsp. crushed red pepper

6 6- to 8-oz. skinless, boneless chicken breast halves

2 cups cauliflower florets

1 large sweet potato (12 oz.), peeled and cut into 1-inch pieces

1 large red sweet pepper, cut into bite-size strips (1 cup)

2 cups hot cooked brown rice

Sliced green onions (optional)

1. Preheat oven to 375°F. In a bowl combine the first six ingredients (through crushed red pepper).

2. Arrange chicken in a 13×9-inch baking pan; brush with half the mustard mixture. Add cauliflower, sweet potato, and sweet pepper; drizzle with remaining mustard mixture.

3. Roast, covered, 25 minutes. Uncover; roast 25 minutes more or until chicken is done (165°F) and sweet potatoes are tender. Serve chicken and vegetables over rice and drizzle with cooking liquid. If desired, top with green onions and additional crushed red pepper.

NUMBER OF SERVINGS 6

*****TIP** If you prefer, omit the honey and Dijon-style mustard and use ½ cup Dijon-style honey mustard.

PER SERVING *429 cal., 10 g fat (2 g sat. fat), 124 mg chol., 353 mg sodium, 42 g carb., 5 g fiber, 16 g sugars, 42 g pro.*

FLEX IT

Substitute six boneless pork loin chops, cut 1 inch thick and trimmed, for the chicken breast halves. Roast until a thermometer registers 145°F.

TURKEY ROASTED WITH BRUSSELS SPROUTS AND CARROTS

PREP 15 minutes **ROAST** 35 minutes at 400°F

Nonstick cooking spray

½ tsp. onion powder

½ tsp. garlic powder

½ tsp. black pepper

½ tsp. salt

1½ lb. turkey breast tenderloins

3 carrots, peeled and cut into bite-size pieces

2 tsp. olive oil

½ cup orange marmalade

1 Tbsp. grated fresh ginger

1 lb. fresh Brussels sprouts, trimmed and halved

Orange wedges

1. Preheat oven to 400°F. Lightly coat a 13×9-inch baking pan with cooking spray. For rub, in a bowl stir together onion powder, garlic powder, pepper, and ¼ tsp. of the salt. Sprinkle evenly over turkey; rub in with your fingers. Place tenderloins on one side of the prepared pan.

2. In a bowl toss carrots with olive oil to coat. Place carrots in opposite side of baking pan. Roast, uncovered, 15 minutes.

3. Meanwhile, in a medium saucepan combine orange marmalade, ginger, and the remaining ¼ tsp. salt. Heat and stir over low heat until melted. Reserve 2 Tbsp. of the marmalade mixture. Add Brussels sprouts to the saucepan; stir to coat. Add Brussels sprouts to carrots in baking pan after 15 minutes of roasting; stir to combine. Brush turkey with reserved marmalade mixture.

4. Roast, uncovered, 20 to 25 minutes more or until turkey is done (165°F) and vegetables are tender, stirring vegetables once. Slice tenderloins and serve with vegetables and orange wedges.

NUMBER OF SERVINGS 6

PER SERVING *260 cal., 3 g fat (1 g sat. fat), 51 mg chol., 325 mg sodium, 31 g carb., 5 g fiber, 21 g sugars, 30 g pro.*

FLEX IT

Turkey breast tenderloins not available? Use 1½ lb. pork tenderloin, trimmed, instead. It's done at 145°F.

SALMON WITH ROASTED TOMATOES AND SHALLOTS

PREP 20 minutes **ROAST** 30 minutes at 400°F

Complete your plate by serving this tomato-topped salmon dish over a bed of hot cooked Israeli couscous tossed with little olive oil and a few handfuls of fresh arugula or baby spinach.

1 1-lb. fresh or frozen salmon fillet, skinned if desired

⅛ tsp. salt

⅛ tsp. black pepper

Nonstick cooking spray

4 cups grape or cherry tomatoes

½ cup thinly sliced shallots

6 cloves garlic, minced

2 Tbsp. snipped fresh oregano or 1½ tsp. dried oregano, crushed

1 Tbsp. olive oil

¼ tsp. salt

¼ tsp. black pepper

1. Preheat oven to 400°F. Thaw salmon, if frozen. Rinse salmon and pat dry. Sprinkle salmon with the ⅛ tsp. salt and pepper.

2. Lightly coat a 3-qt. rectangular baking dish with cooking spray. In the baking dish combine the remaining ingredients. Toss to coat.

3. Roast tomato mixture, uncovered, 15 minutes. Place salmon, skin side down, to the side of tomato mixture. Roast, uncovered, 15 to 18 minutes or until salmon flakes easily.

NUMBER OF SERVINGS 4

PER SERVING *320 cal., 19 g fat (4 g sat. fat), 62 mg chol., 297 mg sodium, 12 g carb., 2 g fiber, 5 g sugars, 26 g pro.*

VEGETABLE-PORK
OVEN STEW
Recipe on page 177

OVEN-LOVIN' STEWS & RAGUS

LATTICE-TOPPED OVEN STEW

PREP 25 minutes **BAKE** 20 minutes at 400°F

Go old-school and serve meat and potatoes made easy with such convenience items as frozen vegetables and refrigerated potatoes and piecrust.

½ 15-oz. pkg. (1 crust) rolled refrigerated unbaked piecrust

1 tsp. sesame seeds

1½ lb. lean ground beef

2 cups refrigerated diced potatoes with onions or loose-pack frozen diced hash brown potatoes with onions and peppers

2 cups loose-pack frozen mixed vegetables

1 15-oz. can Italian-style or regular tomato sauce

1 14.5-oz. can Italian-style stewed tomatoes, undrained

1. Preheat oven to 400°F. Let refrigerated piecrust stand according to package directions. Unfold piecrust. Using a pizza cutter or sharp knife, cut piecrust into ½- to 1-inch-wide strips. Brush strips lightly with water. Sprinkle with sesame seeds.

2. In a large skillet cook ground beef over medium heat until browned. Drain off fat. In a large bowl stir together meat and the remaining ingredients. Spoon into an ungreased 3-qt. rectangular baking dish. Carefully arrange piecrust strips in a lattice pattern on top of meat mixture.

3. Bake, uncovered, 20 to 25 minutes or until heated through and piecrust is golden.

NUMBER OF SERVINGS 8

PER SERVING *335 cal., 15 g fat (6 g sat. fat), 58 mg chol., 686 mg sodium, 30 g carb., 4 g fiber, 5 g sugars, 21 g pro.*

BEEF OVEN STEW

PREP 10 minutes **BAKE** 2 hours at 325°F

4 medium red-skin potatoes, chopped

4 medium carrots, cut into 1-inch pieces, or 2 cups tiny whole carrots

1 cup coarsely chopped onion

½ cup sliced celery

½ cup water or beef broth

2 Tbsp. quick-cooking tapioca

1 lb. beef stew meat, cut into 1-inch cubes

2 14.5-oz. cans stewed tomatoes, undrained, cut up

1 Tbsp. sugar

1 Tbsp. dried Italian seasoning, crushed (optional)

1 tsp. salt

½ tsp. black pepper

1. Preheat oven to 325°F. In a 3-qt. rectangular baking dish combine the first five ingredients (through water). Sprinkle tapioca over vegetables. Add meat. In a bowl combine the remaining ingredients; pour over meat.

2. Bake, covered, 2 hours or until meat is tender. Stir before serving.

NUMBER OF SERVINGS 6

PER SERVING *249 cal., 4 g fat (2 g sat. fat), 48 mg chol., 804 mg sodium, 36 g carb., 5 g fiber, 11 g sugars, 20 g pro.*

Cubed pork shoulder is a delicious option to beef stew meat in this oven-to-table dish.

BEEF STEW POT PIE

PREP 25 minutes **BAKE** 20 minutes at 375°F

When you crave comfort and have little time, reach for cooked beef tips in gravy, a few quick-cooking veggies, and baked croissants to assemble this family favorite.

Nonstick cooking spray

¼ cup butter

3 croissants, split

1½ cups coarsely chopped carrots

1½ cups coarsely chopped celery

1 cup frozen small whole onions, thawed and halved

3 cups sliced fresh mushrooms (8 oz.)

1 cup Burgundy or dry red wine

1 Tbsp. stone-ground Dijon-style mustard

4 cloves garlic, minced

2 tsp. finely snipped fresh rosemary

2 tsp. dried thyme, crushed

½ tsp. black pepper

2 17-oz. pkg. refrigerated cooked beef tips with gravy

1 cup 50%-less-sodium beef broth

1. Preheat oven to 375°F. Coat a 3-qt. rectangular baking dish with cooking spray.

2. In a bowl microwave 1 Tbsp. of the butter on medium high 30 seconds or until melted. Brush cut sides of croissants with melted butter. Cube croissants.

3. In a large skillet melt the remaining 3 Tbsp. butter over medium heat. Add carrots, celery, and onions. Cook 7 to 9 minutes or just until vegetables are tender, stirring occasionally. Carefully stir in the next seven ingredients (through pepper). Bring to boiling; reduce heat. Simmer, uncovered, 5 minutes. Stir in beef with gravy and the broth; heat through.

4. Transfer hot meat mixture to the prepared baking dish. Sprinkle with cubed croissants. Bake, uncovered, 20 to 25 minutes or until bubbly and croissants are golden.

NUMBER OF SERVINGS 8

PER SERVING *330 cal., 16 g fat (8 g sat. fat), 77 mg chol., 885 mg sodium, 21 g carb., 3 g fiber, 8 g sugars, 21 g pro.*

BRAISED BEEF AND CHEDDAR BISCUITS

PREP 30 minutes **COOK** 1 hour **BAKE** 25 minutes at 400°F

- 3 lb. beef stew meat, cut into 1-inch pieces
- 1 14.5-oz. can petite diced tomatoes, undrained
- 1 cup chopped onion
- ½ cup tomato paste
- ⅓ cup dry red wine or beef broth
- ⅓ cup beef broth
- 2 Tbsp. balsamic vinegar
- 6 cloves garlic, minced
- 1 tsp. dried rosemary, crushed
- ½ tsp. salt
- ½ tsp. black pepper
- 12 oz. assorted fresh mushrooms, sliced
- 1 Tbsp. olive oil
- 1 recipe Cheddar Biscuits
  Milk

1. In a 4-qt. Dutch oven combine the first 11 ingredients (through pepper). Bring to boiling; reduce heat. Cover and simmer 1 to 1½ hours or until meat is tender, stirring occasionally.

2. Preheat oven to 400°F. In a large skillet cook mushrooms in hot oil over medium-high heat 6 to 8 minutes or until golden brown, stirring occasionally. Stir into cooked meat mixture.

3. Transfer meat mixture to a 3-qt. rectangular baking dish. Prepare Cheddar Biscuits. On a lightly floured surface pat biscuit dough into a 10×3-inch rectangle and cut into 10 biscuits. Arrange biscuits over meat. Place baking dish on a sturdy baking sheet.

4. Bake, uncovered, 25 to 30 minutes or until golden brown and edges are bubbly and biscuits are golden brown.

NUMBER OF SERVINGS 10

CHEDDAR BISCUITS In a large bowl combine 1½ cups all-purpose flour, 1 tsp. baking powder, and ¼ tsp. salt. Using a pastry blender, cut in ⅓ cup butter, cut up, until mixture resembles coarse crumbs. Make a well in center of flour mixture. In a small bowl beat together ⅓ cup buttermilk and 1 egg. Add buttermilk mixture all at once to flour mixture. Using a fork, stir just until flour mixture is moistened. Stir in ½ cup shredded sharp cheddar cheese (2 oz.). Using floured hands, gently knead dough in bowl until it holds together.

PER SERVING *445 cal., 22 g fat (10 g sat. fat), 119 mg chol., 636 mg sodium, 23 g carb., 2 g fiber, 5 g sugars, 36 g pro.*

SHORT RIB RAGU WITH POLENTA CROUTONS

PREP 45 minutes **BAKE** 2 hours 15 minutes at 325°F + 30 minutes at 375°F **CHILL** 8 hours **BAKE** 1 hour

1 recipe Firm Polenta

3 lb. boneless beef short ribs

Salt and black pepper

2 to 3 Tbsp. olive oil

2 medium onions, thinly sliced

6 cloves garlic, minced

3 medium carrots, halved lengthwise and sliced (1½ cups)

1 cup coarsely chopped celery

1 14-oz. can reduced-sodium beef broth

1½ cups dry red wine

1 6-oz. can tomato paste

4 sprigs fresh thyme

1 8-oz. pkg. cremini mushrooms, quartered (thickly slice larger caps)

1 Tbsp. snipped fresh Italian parsley or basil (optional)

1. Preheat oven to 325°F. Sprinkle ribs with salt and pepper. In a 6- to 8-qt Dutch oven heat 1 Tbsp. of the olive oil over medium heat. Working in batches if necessary, brown ribs in the hot oil, turning to brown all sides; remove ribs and set aside. In the same Dutch oven cook onions and garlic 2 minutes, adding another 1 Tbsp. of the oil if needed. Add carrots and celery; cook 5 minutes more or until vegetables are tender.

2. Return ribs to Dutch oven with the vegetables. Stir in broth, wine, tomato paste, and thyme sprigs. Bring to boiling. Cover; bake 1½ hours. Stir in mushrooms. Bake, uncovered, 45 to 60 minutes more or until ribs are tender and sauce is slightly thickened. Discard thyme sprigs. Season to taste with additional salt and pepper.

3. Increase oven temperature to 375°F. Lightly grease a 3-qt. rectangular baking dish. Skim any fat from surface of the sauce. Spoon ribs and sauce into the prepared baking dish. If desired, cut short ribs into smaller portions. Run a thin metal spatula around the edges of the Firm Polenta in the loaf pan; remove from pan and cut into 1-inch cubes. Arrange cubes over the ribs and sauce in baking dish. Brush cubes with the remaining 1 Tbsp. olive oil.

4. Bake, uncovered, 30 minutes or until polenta is lightly browned. If desired, sprinkle with parsley.

NUMBER OF SERVINGS 8

FIRM POLENTA In a medium saucepan bring 2½ cups water to boiling. In a bowl stir together 1 cup coarse ground cornmeal, 1 cup cold water, and 1 tsp. salt. Slowly add cornmeal mixture to the boiling water, stirring constantly. Cook and stir until mixture returns to boiling. Reduce heat to medium-low (slow boil). Cook 25 to 30 minutes or until mixture is thick, stirring frequently. Pour into an 8×4-inch loaf pan. Cover; chill at least 8 hours or up to 3 days.

PER SERVING 593 cal., 41 g fat (16 g sat. fat), 86 mg chol., 716 mg sodium, 26 g carb., 3 g fiber, 6 g sugars, 22 g pro.

Prepare as directed through Step 2. Transfer ribs to a large airtight container; cover. Chill at least 8 hours or up to 3 days. Continue as directed in Step 3, except bake 1 hour or until ribs are heated through.

COQ AU VIN CASSEROLE

PREP 40 minutes **BAKE** 45 minutes at 350°F

- 2½ to 3 lb. chicken drumsticks and/or thighs, skin removed
- 2 Tbsp. vegetable oil
- Salt and black pepper
- 2 Tbsp. butter
- 3 Tbsp. all-purpose flour
- 1¼ cups Pinot Noir or Burgundy wine
- ¼ cup chicken broth or water
- 1 cup whole fresh mushrooms
- 1 cup thinly sliced carrots
- 18 frozen small whole onions, thawed (⅔ cup)
- 1½ tsp. snipped fresh marjoram or ½ tsp. dried marjoram, crushed
- 1½ tsp. snipped fresh thyme or ½ tsp. dried thyme, crushed
- 2 cloves garlic, minced
- 2 slices bacon, crisp-cooked, drained, and crumbled
- Snipped fresh Italian parsley (optional)
- 3 cups hot cooked noodles (optional)

1. Preheat oven to 350°F. In an extra-large skillet cook chicken, half at a time, in hot oil over medium heat 10 to 15 minutes or until browned, turning occasionally. Transfer chicken to a 3-qt. rectangular baking dish. Sprinkle chicken with salt and pepper.

2. In the same skillet melt butter over medium heat. Stir in flour until smooth. Gradually stir in wine and broth. Cook and stir until sauce comes to boiling. Cut any large mushrooms in half. Stir mushrooms and the next five ingredients (through garlic) into sauce. Return just to boiling. Pour vegetable sauce over chicken.

3. Bake, covered, 45 minutes or until chicken is done (175°F). Top with bacon. If desired, top with parsley and serve with hot cooked noodles.

NUMBER OF SERVINGS 6

PER SERVING *286 cal., 13 g fat (4 g sat. fat), 95 mg chol., 321 mg sodium, 8 g carb., 1 g fiber, 2 g sugars, 24 g pro.*

PORK CASSOULET

PREP 25 minutes **BAKE** 25 minutes at 350°F

1 Tbsp. olive oil

¾ cup chopped onion

¾ cup chopped carrot

¾ cup thinly sliced celery

1½ lb. pork tenderloin, trimmed and cut into 1-inch pieces

8 oz. smoked turkey sausage, thinly sliced

2 15- to 16-oz. cans reduced-sodium Great Northern beans, rinsed and drained

1 cup chopped roma tomatoes

¾ cup reduced-sodium chicken broth

3 Tbsp. tomato paste

1½ tsp. dried Italian seasoning, crushed

3 Tbsp. snipped fresh Italian parsley

1. Preheat oven to 350°F. In a large skillet heat oil over medium heat. Add the onion, carrot, and celery; cook 5 minutes, stirring occasionally. Add pork and sausage; cook 5 minutes more or until browned.

2. In a large bowl mash half of one can of the beans. Stir in the remaining beans and the next four ingredients (through Italian seasoning). Stir into meat mixture. Transfer to a 3-qt. rectangular baking dish.

3. Bake, covered, 25 minutes or until bubbly and pork is tender. Sprinkle with parsley.

NUMBER OF SERVINGS 8

PER SERVING *258 cal., 6 g fat (2 g sat. fat), 70 mg chol., 586 mg sodium, 21 g carb., 5 g fiber, 3 g sugars, 29 g pro.*

MAKE AHEAD

Prepare as directed through Step 2. Cover with heavy foil and chill up to 24 hours. Bake as directed in Step 3, adding about 15 minutes.

VEGETABLE-PORK OVEN STEW

PREP 20 minutes **BAKE** 2 hours 30 minutes at 325°F **COOK** 10 minutes

Easy to assemble, this stew is full of family-favorite veggies. Jazz it up with a bag of red, yellow, and purple potatoes. Cut any large potatoes into 1-inch cubes.

2 Tbsp. vegetable oil

1¾ lb. boneless pork shoulder or pork stew meat, trimmed and cut into 1-inch pieces

1½ cups coarsely chopped onions

2 14.5-oz. cans reduced-sodium chicken broth

1 tsp. dried thyme, crushed

1 tsp. dried oregano, crushed

1 tsp. lemon-pepper seasoning

½ tsp. salt

⅓ cup all-purpose flour

1 16-oz. pkg. frozen whole kernel corn, thawed

1 lb. tiny new potatoes, halved

8 oz. fresh green beans, trimmed and cut into 1½-inch pieces, or 2 cups frozen cut green beans, thawed

1. Preheat oven to 325°F. In an extra-large skillet heat 1 Tbsp. of the oil over medium-high heat. Add two-thirds of the meat and cook about 5 minutes or until browned. Transfer browned meat to 3-qt. rectangular baking dish. Repeat with remaining oil, meat, and onions. Set aside ½ cup of the chicken broth; add remaining chicken broth to the skillet, stirring to release any browned bits from the bottom of skillet. Transfer mixture to the baking dish. Add thyme, oregano, lemon-pepper seasoning, and salt. Cover and bake 1 hour.

2. In a bowl whisk together the reserved ½ cup broth and the flour; stir into stew. Add the corn, potatoes, and beans. Bake, covered, 1½ to 1¾ hours more or until meat and vegetables are tender and mixture is thickened.

NUMBER OF SERVINGS 6

PER SERVING *392 cal., 13 g fat (3 g sat. fat), 79 mg chol., 490 mg sodium, 40 g carb., 6 g fiber, 6 g sugars, 31 g pro.*

GUMBO POT PIE

PREP 40 minutes   **BAKE** 35 minutes at 400°F   **COOK** 10 minutes

Make this gumbo as kickin' or as tame as you like. Use andouille sausage if you like it spicy or kielbasa for a mild stew.

1 lb. fresh or frozen peeled, deveined small shrimp

½ 17.3-oz. pkg. (1 sheet) frozen puff pastry sheets, thawed

½ tsp. Cajun seasoning

1 cup chopped green sweet pepper

1 cup chopped onion

½ cup sliced celery

2 cloves garlic, minced

1 Tbsp. vegetable oil

14 to 16 oz. cooked smoked sausage links, halved lengthwise and sliced

1 14.5-oz. can diced tomatoes, drained

1 10.75-oz. can condensed cream of chicken soup

1 9-oz. pkg. frozen cut okra, thawed

2 Tbsp. tomato paste

½ tsp. salt

¼ tsp. cayenne pepper

1. Thaw shrimp, if frozen. Rinse shrimp and pat dry. Preheat oven to 400°F. Line a baking sheet with parchment paper. Lay pastry sheet on a lightly floured surface. Cut pastry sheet into 2- to 2½-inch squares. Place on prepared baking sheet. Sprinkle top of pastry evenly with Cajun seasoning. Bake 10 minutes.

2. Meanwhile, in an extra-large skillet cook sweet pepper, onion, celery, and garlic in hot oil over medium heat 4 minutes or until vegetables are tender. Stir in the remaining ingredients; heat until bubbly. Add shrimp and return to boiling. Transfer gumbo to a 3-qt. rectangular baking dish.

3. Bake, uncovered, 15 minutes. Place puff pastry squares on the gumbo. Bake 10 minutes more or until gumbo edges are bubbly and pastry is golden brown.

NUMBER OF SERVINGS 10

PER SERVING *377 cal., 25 g fat (7 g sat. fat), 95 mg chol., 938 mg sodium, 21 g carb., 2 g fiber, 4 g sugars, 18 g pro.*

Reduce fat and sodium in this stew by using reduced-fat and reduced-sodium condensed cream of chicken soup and no-salt-added diced tomatoes and tomato paste.

VEGETABLE CURRY

PREP 25 minutes **BAKE** 55 minutes at 350°F

Be sure to use coconut milk—not coconut cream or coconut water—for this recipe. Coconut milk is made from mature coconuts and contains an emulsion of coconut cream and coconut water. It's the workhorse ingredient for Thai recipes.

- 3 cups cauliflower florets
- 1 15-oz. can garbanzo beans (chickpeas), rinsed and drained
- 8 oz. green beans, cut into 1-inch pieces
- 8 oz. new potatoes, quartered
- 1 cup sliced carrots
- ½ cup chopped onion
- ⅓ cup golden raisins (optional)
- 1 Tbsp. curry powder
- ½ tsp. salt
- ¼ tsp. crushed red pepper
- ½ cup reduced-sodium chicken broth or vegetable broth
- 1 cup unsweetened coconut milk
- 3 cups hot cooked basmati or long grain rice
- ¼ cup shredded fresh basil leaves
- ¼ cup chopped cashews or peanuts (optional)

1. Preheat oven to 350°F. In a 3-qt. rectangular baking dish combine the first 10 ingredients (through crushed red pepper). Drizzle with broth. Cover and bake 45 minutes.

2. Drizzle with coconut milk. Bake, uncovered, 10 minutes more or until vegetables are tender and sauce thickens slightly. Serve curry over rice. Top with basil and, if desired, cashews.

NUMBER OF SERVINGS 6

PER SERVING *298 cal., 8 g fat (6 g sat. fat), 0 mg chol., 375 mg sodium, 49 g carb., 7 g fiber, 6 g sugars, 8 g pro.*

FLEX IT

If you have leftover cooked chicken, stir 2 cups cubed chicken breast into the vegetable mixture along with the coconut milk in Step 2.

**ITALIAN ROAST
BEEF SLIDER MELTS**
Recipe on page 193

SANDWICHES, SLIDERS & PIZZAS

CRISPY CHICKEN-BACON SANDWICHES

PREP 30 minutes **BAKE** 15 minutes at 425°F

A little canned chipotle adds a smoky punch, but what to do with leftovers? Here's an idea: Spread remaining chiles in a resealable plastic freezer bag; seal and freeze flat. Next time a recipe calls for it, break off as much as you need.

2 Tbsp. light mayonnaise

½ tsp. finely chopped canned chipotle chile peppers in adobo sauce*

½ tsp. sugar

½ tsp. lime juice

Nonstick cooking spray

2 skinless, boneless chicken breast halves (about 1 lb. total)

¼ cup plain fat-free Greek yogurt

1 Tbsp. water

½ cup soft whole wheat bread crumbs

¼ cup regular rolled oats

3 Tbsp. finely chopped dried cherries

4 whole wheat sandwich thins, toasted

Spinach or lettuce leaves

4 slices tomato

8 slices lower-sodium, less-fat bacon, cooked

1. In a bowl stir together mayonnaise, chile peppers, sugar, and lime juice.

2. Preheat oven to 425°F. Line a 13×9-inch baking pan with foil; coat foil with cooking spray. Cut chicken breasts in half lengthwise. In a shallow dish stir together yogurt and the water. In another shallow dish combine bread crumbs, oats, and dried cherries. Dip chicken pieces in yogurt mixture, turning to coat. Dip in bread crumb mixture, turning to coat evenly.

3. Place chicken in the prepared baking pan. Bake 15 to 18 minutes or until chicken is no longer pink (165°F) and outside is golden brown.

4. Spread mayonnaise mixture on cut sides of sandwich thin tops. Layer with spinach, chicken, tomato, and bacon. Add tops.

NUMBER OF SERVINGS 4

*TIP Chile peppers contain oils that can irritate your skin and eyes. Wear plastic or rubber gloves when working with them.

PER SANDWICH *348 cal., 9 g fat (2 g sat. fat), 91 mg chol., 457 mg sodium, 30 g carb., 6 g fiber, 4 g sugars, 37 g pro.*

HAM, CHEESE, AND TURKEY STROMBOLI

PREP 20 minutes **BAKE** 30 minutes at 375°F

This versatile stuffed sandwich can be served for brunch or dinner, or as an appetizer. Or wrap the sandwich in foil, tuck it an insulated carrier, and take it to your next tailgate.

1 tsp. olive oil

1 Tbsp. cornmeal

1 13.8-oz. pkg. refrigerated pizza dough

4 oz. thinly sliced cooked ham

1 cup shredded mozzarella cheese (4 oz.)

1 cup fresh baby spinach or torn spinach leaves

4 oz. thinly sliced cooked turkey

⅓ cup chopped red, green, or yellow sweet pepper

¼ cup Kalamata olives, pitted and chopped

1 egg, lightly beaten

Marinara sauce or pizza sauce (optional)

1. Preheat oven to 375°F. Lightly brush a 13×9-inch baking pan with oil; sprinkle with cornmeal.

2. On a lightly floured surface, carefully stretch or roll pizza dough into a 13×10-inch rectangle. Arrange ham slices on dough to within ½ inch of the edges. Sprinkle with ½ cup of the cheese. Layer spinach and turkey on cheese. Top with the remaining ½ cup cheese, the sweet pepper, and olives. Starting from a long side, roll up dough; pinch to seal seams.

3. Place loaf, seam side down, in the prepared baking pan. Brush with egg; cut a few slits in top for steam to escape. Bake 30 minutes or until golden brown. Cool slightly.

4. Cut into eight slices. If desired, serve with marinara sauce.

NUMBER OF SERVINGS 4

PER 2 SLICES *417 cal., 17 g fat (5 g sat. fat), 93 mg chol., 1,290 mg sodium, 44 g carb., 3 g fiber, 3 g sugars, 23 g pro.*

EGG BAGUETTE BAKE

PREP 30 minutes **BAKE** 35 minutes at 350°F **STAND** 5 minutes

1 1-lb. Italian or French baguette (unsliced) (12×4-inch)

4 oz. sweet or mild Italian sausage

⅓ cup chopped red or yellow sweet pepper

¼ cup sliced green onions

5 eggs, lightly beaten

⅓ cup heavy cream or half-and-half

½ cup snipped fresh basil

¼ tsp. salt

¾ cup shredded Fontina, mozzarella, or provolone cheese (3 oz.)

1. Preheat oven to 350°F. Line a 13×9-inch baking pan with parchment paper. Using a serrated knife, cut a wedge into the top of the loaf, cutting to about 1 inch from each long side. Use a spoon or your fingers to carefully remove the inside of loaf, leaving about ¾-inch shell. (Save interior bread for making croutons or use in meat loaf.) Place bread shell in the prepared baking pan.

2. Remove casing from sausage, if present. In a large skillet crumble and cook sausage with sweet pepper for 8 minutes or just until sausage is cooked and pepper is tender, stirring in the green onions the last 1 minute of cooking. Remove from heat; drain off fat.

3. In a large bowl combine eggs, cream, basil, and salt. Stir in sausage mixture and ½ cup of the cheese.

4. Carefully pour egg mixture into bread shell. Sprinkle with the remaining ¼ cup cheese. Bake 35 to 40 minutes or until eggs are set (160°F). Let stand 5 minutes. Using a serrated knife, carefully cut loaf into slices.

NUMBER OF SERVINGS 5

PER SLICE *490 cal., 23 g fat (11 g sat. fat), 245 mg chol., 977 mg sodium, 45 g carb., 0 g fiber, 1 g sugars, 20 g pro.*

To reduce fat in this egg bake, use turkey sausage; 1¼ cups refrigerated or frozen egg product, thawed; and part-skim mozzarella cheese.

Omit the meat yet keep the meatiness. Substitute 1 cup sliced fresh mushrooms for the sausage. Shiitake or portobello mushrooms are especially good. Cook them in 2 tsp. olive oil along with the sweet pepper.

MANDARIN BEEF BUNS

PREP 35 minutes **RISE** 20 minutes **BAKE** 15 minutes at 375°F

1 Tbsp. vegetable oil

2 cups shredded cooked beef or pork

¼ tsp. crushed red pepper

1 cup chopped bok choy, napa cabbage, or green cabbage

2 Tbsp. grated fresh ginger

1 tsp. orange zest

⅓ cup thinly bias-sliced green onions

¼ cup hoisin sauce

1 16-oz. pkg. hot roll mix

1 egg, lightly beaten

Sesame seeds

1. For filling, in a large skillet heat oil over medium heat. Add meat and crushed red pepper; cook 3 minutes. Add bok choy, ginger, and orange zest; cook 2 to 3 minutes or until bok choy is wilted. Stir in green onions and hoisin sauce. Let cool.

2. Prepare the hot roll mix according to package directions. Divide dough into 24 portions. Roll each portion into a ball. On a lightly floured surface, roll or pat each ball into a 3½-inch circle.

3. For each bun, place about 1 Tbsp. of the filling in center of each circle. Moisten edges of dough with water and bring up around filling, pinching edges together to seal.

4. Arrange the filled buns, seam sides down, in two lightly greased 13×9-inch baking pans. Cover and let rise in a warm place 20 minutes.

5. Preheat oven to 375°F. Brush buns with egg; sprinkle with sesame seeds. Bake 15 minutes or until golden.

NUMBER OF SERVINGS 12

PER 2 BUNS *201 cal., 5 g fat (1 g sat. fat), 31 mg chol., 379 mg sodium, 29 g carb., 1 g fiber, 4 g sugars, 11 g pro.*

MAKE AHEAD

Prepare and bake buns as directed. Cool 30 minutes. Wrap buns in heavy foil and freeze up to 1 month. To reheat, leave the frozen buns in foil. Bake in a 325°F oven 40 minutes or until heated through.

SWEET-SPICY BARBECUED CHICKEN SLIDERS

PREP 35 minutes **BAKE** 25 minutes at 350°F

12 3-inch sandwich rolls, split

2½ cups shredded cooked
chicken breast

1 cup chopped fresh or
canned pineapple, well
drained

⅔ cup barbecue sauce

¼ cup chopped pickled
jalapeño peppers

1½ cups shredded Monterrey
Jack cheese (6 oz.)

6 Tbsp. melted butter

2 Tbsp. honey

1 Tbsp. Worcestershire sauce

½ tsp. black pepper

Sliced fresh jalapeño chile
peppers (tip, page 184)
(optional)

1. Preheat oven to 350°F. Arrange bottoms of rolls in a 13×9-inch baking pan or 3-qt. rectangular baking dish. In a bowl combine the next four ingredients (through pickled jalapeño peppers). Spoon onto roll bottoms. Top with cheese and roll tops.

2. In a bowl combine the next four ingredients (through black pepper). Drizzle over rolls. Cover pan with foil.

3. Bake 15 minutes. Uncover; bake 10 to 15 minutes more or until cheese is melted and roll tops are lightly browned.

NUMBER OF SERVINGS 12

PER SANDWICH *390 cal., 15 g fat (7 g sat. fat), 71 mg chol., 603 mg sodium, 40 g carb., 1 g fiber, 12 g sugars, 23 g pro.*

Assemble the sandwiches but do not drizzle with butter mixture. Cover with foil and refrigerate up to 8 hours. Then drizzle and bake as directed in Step 3.

ITALIAN ROAST BEEF SLIDER MELTS

PREP 35 minutes **BAKE** 25 minutes at 350°F

- 12 3-inch sourdough rolls, split
- 12 oz. thinly sliced deli-style roast beef
- 1½ cups chopped pickled mixed vegetables (giardiniera)
- 6 oz. thinly sliced provolone or mozzarella cheese
- 1 8-oz. tub cream cheese spread with garden vegetables
- ¼ cup olive oil
- 2 cloves garlic, minced
- 1 tsp. dried Italian seasoning, crushed
- ½ tsp. crushed red pepper

1. Preheat oven to 350°F. Arrange bottoms of rolls in a 13×9-inch baking pan or 3-qt. rectangular baking dish. Layer roll bottoms with roast beef, pickled mixed vegetables, and provolone. Spread cut sides of roll tops with cream cheese' add roll tops.

2. In a bowl combine the remaining ingredients. Drizzle over rolls. Cover pan with foil.

3. Bake 15 minutes. Uncover; bake 10 to 15 minutes more or until cheese is melted and roll tops are lightly browned.

NUMBER OF SERVINGS 12

PER SANDWICH *362 cal., 16 g fat (7 g sat. fat), 51 mg chol., 881 mg sodium, 35 g carb., 1 g fiber, 4 g sugars, 19 g pro.*

Assemble sandwiches but do not drizzle with olive oil mixture. Cover with foil and refrigerate up to 8 hours. Drizzle and bake as directed in Step 3.

VEGGIE REUBEN PRETZEL MELTS

PREP 35 minutes **BAKE** 25 minutes at 350°F

Nonstick cooking spray

12 3-inch pretzel rolls, split

2 cups fresh baby spinach

1 cup thinly sliced well-drained roasted red peppers

½ cup thinly sliced red onion

½ cup thinly sliced cucumber

1 cup well-drained sauerkraut

6 oz. thinly sliced Swiss cheese

½ cup Thousand Island dressing

6 Tbsp. butter, melted

1 Tbsp. coarse-ground mustard

1 tsp. crushed caraway seeds

½ tsp. minced dried onion

1. Preheat oven to 350°F. Line a 13×9-inch baking pan or 3-qt. rectangular baking dish with foil. Coat with cooking spray. Arrange roll bottoms in prepared pan.

2. Layer the next six ingredients (through Swiss cheese) on bottoms of rolls. Spread dressing on cut sides of roll tops. Add roll tops to sandwiches. In a bowl stir together the remaining ingredients; drizzle over sandwiches. Cover pan with foil.

3. Bake 15 minutes. Uncover; bake 10 to 15 minutes more or until cheese is melted and roll tops are lightly browned.

NUMBER OF SERVINGS 12

PER SANDWICH *367 cal., 19 g fat (7 g sat. fat), 31 mg chol., 644 mg sodium, 40 g carb., 2 g fiber, 5 g sugars, 10 g pro.*

Turn these veggie-filled sandwiches into traditional Reubens or Rachels by adding thinly sliced corned beef or turkey.

Assemble the sandwiches but do not drizzle with butter mixture. Cover with foil and refrigerate up to 8 hours. Drizzle and bake as directed in Step 3.

MAKE-IT-MINE DEEP-DISH PIZZA

PREP 20 minutes **BAKE** 20 minutes at 400°F

Involve the family in making this easy weeknight-friendly pizza. Start with purchased pizza dough, then pick from three hearty fillings. Choose one or two cheeses, then set out toppings for everyone to choose.

BASE RECIPE

Cornmeal

1 13.8-oz. pkg. refrigerated plain pizza dough or pizza dough with multigrain

Filling

1½ cups shredded Cheese (6 oz.)

¾ cup shredded Parmesan cheese (3 oz.)

Toppings

1. Preheat oven to 400°F. Lightly grease a 13×9-inch baking pan and sprinkle lightly with cornmeal. On a lightly floured surface, unroll pizza dough. Cut 4 inches crosswise from the rectangle and set aside. Roll remaining dough into a 13×9-inch rectangle. Transfer to the prepared baking pan; press edges to form a crust.

2. Spread Filling evenly over crust in pan. Sprinkle with desired Cheese. Cut remaining dough into random-size strips and pieces; arrange on top of filling. Sprinkle with Parmesan.

3. Bake, uncovered, 20 to 25 minutes or until golden and bubbly. Add desired Toppings.

NUMBER OF SERVINGS 8

FILLING

* **Sausage-Spinach** In a medium bowl stir together 8 oz. bulk hot or sweet Italian sausage, cooked, crumbled, and drained; half a 10-oz. pkg. frozen chopped spinach, thawed and squeezed dry; 1 cup pizza sauce or pasta sauce; one 6-oz. jar marinated artichoke hearts, drained and chopped; ½ cup sliced pitted ripe olives or Kalamata olives; and ⅓ cup slivered red onion.

* **Buffalo Chicken** Stir together 3 cups shredded cooked chicken, 1 cup crumbled blue cheese (4 oz.), ¾ cup buffalo wing sauce, and ½ cup sliced green onions. If desired, top pizza with additional sliced green onions and crumbled blue cheese.

* **Baked Potato** Stir together one 20-oz. pkg. refrigerated diced potatoes with onions, cooked according to package directions; one 15-oz. jar Alfredo pasta sauce; 8 oz. ground beef, cooked, crumbled, and drained; and 6 slices bacon, crisp-cooked and crumbled.

CHEESE

* Cheddar cheese
* Italian-blend cheeses
* Mexican-style four-cheese blend
* Monterey Jack cheese
* Mozzarella cheese
* Provolone cheese

TOPPINGS

* Crumbled crisp-cooked bacon
* Hot pepper sauce
* Ranch or blue cheese salad dressing
* Sliced pepperoncini salad peppers
* Snipped fresh chives, basil, or oregano
* Sliced green onions
* Sliced pitted ripe or Kalamata olives
* Sour cream

MOROCCAN-SPICED DEEP-DISH PIZZA

PREP 30 minutes **BAKE** 25 minutes at 425°F **STAND** 15 minutes

1 lb. purchased pizza dough

1 Tbsp. olive oil

2 Tbsp. cornmeal

8 oz. bulk spicy pork or turkey sausage

1 24-oz. jar pasta sauce

1 recipe Moroccan Spice Mix

3 cups shredded mozzarella cheese (12 oz.)

2 cups sliced cremini mushrooms

1 medium green sweet pepper, cut in thin strips

1 medium onion, sliced

¼ cup grated Parmesan cheese (optional)

1. Preheat oven to 425°F. On a lightly floured surface roll dough to a 14×10-inch rectangle. Brush bottom and sides of a 13×9-inch baking pan with olive oil. Sprinkle bottom of pan with cornmeal. Place dough in pan, pressing dough ½ inch up sides of pan. Cover.

2. In a large skillet brown sausage over medium heat. Drain off fat. Stir in pasta sauce and Moroccan Spice Mix. Bring to boiling; reduce heat. Simmer, uncovered, 7 to 10 minutes or until thickened, stirring occasionally.

3. Layer half the mozzarella, mushrooms, sweet pepper, and onion over dough in pan. Spoon sauce over top. Top with remaining mozzarella, vegetables, and Parmesan (pan will be full).

4. Bake, uncovered, 25 to 30 minutes or until crust is browned and filling is bubbly. Let stand 15 minutes. Cut into eight squares.

NUMBER OF SERVINGS 8

MOROCCAN SPICE MIX In a small jar combine 2 tsp. ground turmeric; 1 tsp. each ground cumin and ground coriander; ¾ tsp. each paprika and garlic powder; ½ tsp. dried thyme, crushed; and ⅛ tsp. cayenne pepper. Cover and store in a cool, dark place up to 6 months.

PER SQUARE *414 cal., 18 g fat (7 g sat. fat), 47 mg chol., 983 mg sodium, 41 g carb., 4 g fiber, 9 g sugars, 22 g pro.*

FLEX IT

Make this deep-dish pizza a little more authentic (and vegetarian) by substituting one 15-oz. can garbanzo beans (chickpeas), rinsed and drained, for the sausage in Step 2.

BRUSSELS SPROUTS AND FENNEL SAUSAGE PIZZA

PREP 35 minutes **BAKE** 25 minutes at 425°F **STAND** 15 minutes

These are not conventional pizza toppings, but they work together deliciously. The DIY Italian sausage is layered with nutty Gruyère cheese and healthful Brussels sprouts.

1 lb. purchased pizza dough

3 Tbsp. olive oil

2 Tbsp. cornmeal

12 oz. uncooked ground pork

1 tsp. fennel seeds

½ to 1 tsp. crushed red pepper

½ tsp. salt

8 oz. Gruyère cheese, shredded (2 cups)

8 oz. Brussels sprouts, trimmed and sliced

1 small red onion, thinly sliced and separated into rings

4 cloves garlic, minced

1. Preheat oven to 425°F. On a lightly floured surface roll dough to a 14×10-inch rectangle. Brush the bottom and sides of a 13×9-inch baking pan with 2 Tbsp of the olive oil. Sprinkle bottom of pan with cornmeal. Place dough in pan, pressing dough ½ inch up sides of pan. Cover and let rest 10 minutes.

2. Meanwhile, in a bowl combine pork, fennel seeds, crushed red pepper, and salt. In a large skillet cook pork mixture over medium-high heat until no longer pink. Drain off fat.

3. Press crust up sides of pan if it has fallen. Top with cheese, cooked pork, Brussels sprouts, onion, and garlic. Drizzle with the remaining 1 Tbsp. oil. Bake 25 to 30 minutes or until crust and filling have browned. Let stand 15 minutes. Loosen crust and slide pizza out of pan. Cut into eight squares.

NUMBER OF SERVINGS 8

PER SQUARE *439 cal., 24 g fat (9 g sat. fat), 65 mg chol., 647 mg sodium, 32 g carb., 2 g fiber, 3 g sugars, 24 g pro.*

**ROASTED ROOT VEGETABLE
AND ROMAINE SALAD**
Recipe on page 213

VEGGIE FRESH

ROASTED TOMATO AND BREAD TOSS

PREP 15 minutes **ROAST** 20 minutes at 400°F

For richer flavor, substitute balsamic glaze for the balsamic vinegar. Bottled balsamic glaze has become a popular condiment and is found near vinegars in supermarkets.

2 lb. cherry or grape tomatoes (about 6 cups)

6 cups torn baguette or Italian bread (12 oz.)

2 to 3 Tbsp. olive oil

½ cup pitted Kalamata and/or green olives

2 Tbsp. olive oil

2 Tbsp. balsamic vinegar

4 cloves garlic, minced

½ tsp. kosher salt

½ tsp. freshly ground black pepper

1. Position one oven rack in the upper third of the oven. Preheat oven to 400°F. Line a 13×9-inch baking pan with parchment paper. Arrange tomatoes in a single layer in the prepared pan. Place bread in large bowl. Drizzle 2 to 3 Tbsp. olive oil over bread pieces. Toss to coat. In a second 13×9-inch baking pan arrange bread in a single layer.

2. Roast tomatoes on upper rack and bread on lower rack for 20 to 25 minutes or just until skins on tomatoes begin to split and wrinkle and bread is lightly toasted, stirring once.

3. Add bread and olives to tomatoes in pan; gently toss to combine. In a bowl whisk together the remaining ingredients. Drizzle vinegar mixture over tomatoes, olives, and bread. Toss to coat.

NUMBER OF SERVINGS 8

PER SERVING *215 cal., 10 g fat (1 g sat. fat), 0 mg chol., 494 mg sodium, 28 g carb., 3 g fiber, 5 g sugars, 5 g pro.*

FLEX IT

Turn this warm salad into a main dish by adding 1 lb. cooked peeled and deveined shrimp with the bread.

VEGETARIAN LASAGNA

PREP 45 minutes **BAKE** 45 minutes at 375°F **STAND** 20 minutes

3 large bunches Swiss chard, rinsed and drained (1½ to 2 lb. total)

3 cloves garlic, minced

1 Tbsp. olive oil

1 tsp. kosher salt

¼ tsp. ground nutmeg

12 dried lasagna noodles*

12 oz. goat cheese (chèvre), room temperature

½ cup milk

1 egg

2 Tbsp. snipped fresh chives

Olive oil

4 cups cherry tomatoes, halved

1 cup coarsely chopped walnuts

¼ cup grated Parmesan cheese

1. Preheat oven to 375°F. Remove and discard thick stems from Swiss chard; coarsely chop leaves. In a large Dutch oven cook garlic in hot oil 30 seconds over medium heat. Add Swiss chard in batches. Cook 2 minutes or until all the chard is slightly wilted. Sprinkle with ½ tsp. of the salt and the nutmeg; set aside.

2. Cook noodles according to package directions until tender but still firm (al dente). Drain; rinse with cold water. Drain well.

3. For filling, in a bowl whisk together goat cheese, milk, egg, chives, and the remaining ½ tsp. salt until well combined.

4. Drizzle the bottom of a 3-qt. rectangular baking dish with olive oil. Arrange 3 noodles in a single layer on oil. Layer with one-fourth of the filling, one-fourth of the Swiss chard mixture, one-fourth of the cherry tomatoes, and one-fourth of the walnuts. Repeat layers three more times. Sprinkle top with Parmesan cheese. Cover with a piece of parchment paper brushed with olive oil, coated side down; seal tightly with foil.

5. Bake 30 minutes. Uncover; bake 15 minutes more or until cheese is golden and mixture is bubbly. Let stand 20 minutes before serving.

NUMBER OF SERVINGS 8

*TIP Because this lasagna has a thick sauce, don't use no-boil noodles.

PER SERVING *468 cal., 28 g fat (11 g sat. fat), 60 mg chol., 708 mg sodium, 35 g carb., 5 g fiber, 6 g sugars, 21 g pro.*

MAKE AHEAD

Prepare as directed through Step 1. Store wilted Swiss chard in the refrigerator up to 3 days.

ROASTED VEGETABLES AND CHICKPEAS

PREP 30 minutes   **ROAST** 45 minutes at 425°F

Roasting vegetables at a high temperature until browned draws out their natural flavors and sweetness. Finish with a few simple seasonings.

1 lb. carrots, peeled and cut into 2-inch pieces

1 lb. sweet potatoes, peeled and cut into chunks

1 large red onion, peeled, halved, and cut into 1-inch wedges

1 lb. red or russet potatoes, cubed

6 cloves garlic, minced

1 16-oz. can garbanzo beans (chickpeas), rinsed and drained

2 to 3 Tbsp. vegetable oil or olive oil

1 tsp. dried rosemary, crushed

1 tsp. packed brown sugar or granulated sugar

½ tsp. kosher salt

½ tsp. black pepper

Snipped fresh rosemary (optional)

1. Position an oven rack in center of oven. Preheat oven to 425°F. Place the first six ingredients (through chickpeas) in a 13×9-inch pan. In a bowl whisk together the next five ingredients (through pepper). Drizzle over vegetables; toss to coat.

2. Roast, uncovered, 45 minutes or until vegetables are lightly browned and tender, stirring twice. If desired, sprinkle with snipped fresh rosemary.

NUMBER OF SERVINGS 8

PER SERVING *223 cal., 4 g fat (0 g sat. fat), 0 mg chol., 301 mg sodium, 42 g carb., 7 g fiber, 9 g sugars, 6 g pro.*

MASHED BAKED POTATOES WITH GARDEN CONFETTI

PREP 35 minutes   **BAKE** 45 minutes at 425°F + 2 hours at 325°F   **CHILL** 2 hours

Nonstick cooking spray

5 lb. red-skin potatoes (about 15 medium)

1 8-oz. pkg. regular or reduced-fat cream cheese (neufchatel), cut up and softened

1 tsp. salt

1 tsp. cracked black pepper

1½ cups half-and-half or evaporated fat-free milk

1 recipe Garden Confetti

2 Tbsp. butter, melted

1. Preheat oven to 425°F. Coat a 3-qt. rectangular baking dish with cooking spray. Scrub potatoes thoroughly with a brush; pat dry. Prick potatoes with a fork. Bake 45 to 60 minutes or until tender.

2. Transfer half the potatoes to an extra-large bowl. (Cut any large potatoes in half or quarters.) Mash potatoes until slightly lumpy; transfer to a large bowl. Use the same extra-large bowl to mash the remaining potatoes.

3. Return all the potatoes to the extra-large bowl; add cream cheese, salt, and pepper. Gradually beat in half-and-half until mashed potatoes are light and fluffy. Transfer mashed potatoes to the prepared baking dish. Top with Garden Confetti; drizzle with melted butter. Cover with foil. Chill at least 2 hours.

4. Preheat oven to 325°F. Bake, covered, 1 hour. Bake, uncovered, 1 to 1¼ hours more or until heated through.

NUMBER OF SERVINGS 10

GARDEN CONFETTI In a large skillet melt 3 Tbsp. butter over medium-high heat. Add 1½ cups shredded carrots; 1 medium onion, halved and thinly sliced; ½ cup each finely chopped red sweet pepper and finely chopped green sweet pepper; and 2 cloves garlic, minced. Cook and stir 4 to 5 minutes or until vegetables are tender. If desired, stir in 1 tsp. snipped fresh rosemary or thyme.

PER SERVING *350 cal., 18 g fat (11 g sat. fat), 51 mg chol., 426 mg sodium, 43 g carb., 5 g fiber, 7 g sugars, 7 g pro.*

Prepare as directed through Step 3. Cover and refrigerate up to 24 hours. Continue as directed.

STUFFED NEW POTATOES

PREP 25 minutes **BAKE** 1 hour + 2 minutes at 425°F **STAND** 10 minutes

12 small red potatoes
(about 4 lb. total)

½ cup sour cream

¼ cup snipped fresh chives

1 Tbsp. Dijon-style mustard

1 tsp. salt

1 tsp. smoked paprika

¾ cup finely shredded Swiss,
provolone, or cheddar
cheese (3 oz.)

Snipped fresh chives
(optional)

1. Preheat oven to 425°F. Scrub potatoes thoroughly with a brush; pat dry. Prick potatoes with a fork. Bake 45 to 60 minutes or until tender. Let stand about 10 minutes or until cool enough to handle.

2. Cut a slice off the top of each baked potato;* discard skin from slices and place pulp in a bowl. If necessary, cut a small slice off bottoms of potatoes so they stand upright. Using a melon baller, scoop out pulp from potatoes; add pulp to the bowl. Set potato shells aside.

3. Mash the potato pulp. Add the next five ingredients (through paprika). Stir in ½ cup of the cheese. Spoon mashed potato into potato shells. Place filled shells in a 13×9-inch baking pan.

4. Bake, uncovered, 15 to 20 minutes or until lightly browned. Sprinkle with the remaining ¼ cup cheese. Bake 2 to 3 minutes more or until cheese is melted. If desired, sprinkle with chives.

NUMBER OF SERVINGS 12

*__TIP__ If the potatoes are on the large side, cut them in half crosswise.

PER SERVING 153 cal., 4 g fat (2 g sat. fat), 12 mg chol., 254 mg sodium, 25 g carb., 3 g fiber, 2 g sugars, 5 g pro.

ROASTED ROOT VEGETABLE AND ROMAINE SALAD

PREP 15 minutes **ROAST** 30 minutes at 375°F

1½ lb. carrots, turnips, and/or parsnips

2 small shallots, peeled and quartered

3 Tbsp. olive oil

¼ tsp. salt

Black pepper

1 medium pear, cored and coarsely chopped

2 Tbsp. white wine vinegar

1½ tsp. snipped fresh thyme

½ tsp. Dijon-style mustard

½ tsp. honey

1 clove garlic, minced

4 cups torn romaine lettuce

¼ cup coarsely chopped pecans, toasted (tip, page 21)

1 Tbsp. coarsely chopped fresh Italian parsley

1. Preheat oven to 375°F. Peel carrots and bias-cut into 1-inch lengths. (If using turnips, cut into 1-inch pieces.) Place in a 13×9-inch baking pan. Add shallots. Toss with 1 Tbsp. of the olive oil. Sprinkle with ⅛ tsp. of the salt and pepper to taste.

2. Roast, uncovered, 15 minutes. Stir in pear. Roast 15 minutes more or until vegetables are tender. Cool slightly.

3. Meanwhile, for dressing, in a screw-top jar combine the remaining 2 Tbsp. olive oil and ⅛ tsp. salt and the next five ingredients (through garlic); add pepper to taste. Cover and shake well.

4. In a bowl combine lettuce and dressing; toss to coat. Transfer to a platter. Top with roasted vegetable mixture. Sprinkle with pecans and parsley.

NUMBER OF SERVINGS 6

PER SERVING *168 cal., 10 g fat (1 g sat. fat), 0 mg chol., 189 mg sodium, 19 g carb., 5 g fiber, 10 g sugars, 2 g pro.*

Prepare as directed through Step 3. Cool vegetable mixture. Place in an airtight container; cover. Refrigerate vegetable mixture and dressing up to 3 days. Before serving, bring to room temperature. Serve as directed.

EDAMAME, CORN, AND CHEESE ENCHILADAS

PREP 20 minutes **BAKE** 35 minutes at 350°F

Nonstick cooking spray

1 cup frozen edamame, thawed, or canned black or pinto beans, rinsed and drained

1 cup frozen whole kernel corn, thawed

2 tsp. fajita seasoning

2 cups shredded Monterey Jack cheese (8 oz.)

10 7- to 8-inch whole wheat flour tortillas

1 15-oz. can tomato sauce

1 14.5-oz. can fire-roasted or regular diced tomatoes, undrained

1½ to 2 tsp. chili powder

Snipped fresh cilantro

1. Preheat oven to 350°F. Coat a 3-qt. rectangular baking dish with cooking spray. In a bowl combine edamame, corn, and fajita seasoning. Stir in 1½ cups of the cheese. Spoon about ⅓ cup of the mixture onto each tortilla; roll up. Place, seam sides down, in the prepared dish.

2. In a bowl stir together tomato sauce, tomatoes, and chili powder; pour over filled tortillas.

3. Bake, covered, 20 minutes. Uncover; bake 15 to 20 minutes more or until heated through, sprinkling with remaining ½ cup cheese the last 5 minutes. Top with cilantro and, if desired, additional chili powder.

NUMBER OF SERVINGS 10

PER SERVING *269 cal., 11 g fat (5 g sat. fat), 20 mg chol., 759 mg sodium, 32 g carb., 5 g fiber, 6 g sugars, 13 g pro.*

 FLEX IT

Watching your sodium intake?
Use no-salt-added tomato sauce
and diced tomatoes.

FOUR-CHEESE ZUCCHINI STRATA

PREP 35 minutes **CHILL** 2 hours **BAKE** 45 minutes at 325°F **STAND** 10 minutes

2 Tbsp. olive oil

4 medium zucchini, halved lengthwise and cut into ¼-inch pieces (about 5 cups)

8 cups Italian flatbread with garlic (focaccia), cut into bite-size pieces

1 cup shredded provolone cheese (4 oz.)

1 cup shredded white cheddar cheese (4 oz.)

½ cup crumbled blue cheese (2 oz.)

½ cup grated Parmesan cheese

7 eggs, lightly beaten

2 cups milk

2 Tbsp. snipped fresh parsley

½ tsp. salt

½ tsp. black pepper

1. Grease a 3-qt. rectangular baking dish. In an extra-large skillet heat oil over medium-high heat. Add zucchini; cook until zucchini is lightly browned, stirring occasionally. Remove from heat.

2. Arrange half the bread pieces in the prepared baking dish. Top with half the zucchini and half of each of the cheeses. Repeat layers. In a bowl combine eggs, milk, parsley, salt, and pepper. Pour evenly over layers in baking dish. Cover dish with plastic wrap. Chill at least 2 hours.

3. Preheat oven to 325°F. Remove plastic wrap. Bake, uncovered, 45 to 50 minutes or until center is set and a thermometer inserted in center registers 170°F. Let stand 10 minutes before serving.

NUMBER OF SERVINGS 8

PER SERVING 347 cal., 23 g fat (11 g sat. fat), 228 mg chol., 742 mg sodium, 16 g carb., 1 g fiber, 5 g sugars, 22 g pro.

MAKE AHEAD

Prepare as directed through Step 2. Cover and refrigerate strata up to 24 hours. Bake as directed.

HEALTHY CHOICE

To reduce fat in this strata, substitute 1¾ cups refrigerated or frozen egg product, thawed, for the whole eggs and substitute reduced-fat cheeses.

OVEN-COOKED SWISS CHARD

PREP 20 minutes **BAKE** 20 minutes at 350°F

Swiss chard is a hearty green that can hold up to cooking in the oven. Cook it alongside beef,
lamb, or pork roast to serve as a bed for the meat or as a side dish.

1 bunch Swiss chard (about
   1 lb.), rinsed

¼ cup golden raisins

3 Tbsp. olive oil

2 Tbsp. balsamic vinegar

¼ tsp. salt

¼ tsp. black pepper

¼ cup pine nuts or slivered
   almonds, toasted (tip,
   page 21) (optional)

1. Preheat oven to 350°F. Slice Swiss chard leaves into 2-inch pieces and chop stems into ¾-inch pieces.

2. In a large bowl combine chard, raisins, and oil; toss gently to coat. Transfer to an ungreased 3-qt. rectangular baking dish, mounding slightly in center if necessary.

3. Bake, covered, 20 to 25 minutes or until chard is slightly wilted. Add vinegar, salt, and pepper; toss gently to coat. Transfer to a serving dish. If desired, sprinkle with pine nuts.

NUMBER OF SERVINGS 6

PER SERVING *132 cal., 11 g fat (1 g sat. fat), 0 mg chol., 259 mg sodium, 9 g carb., 2 g fiber, 5 g sugars, 2 g pro.*

BROWN SUGAR–CHILE BAKED ACORN SQUASH

PREP 25 minutes **BAKE** 1 hour 15 minutes at 350°F

- 3 small acorn squash (14 to 16 oz. each), halved lengthwise and seeded
- ⅓ cup packed brown sugar
- ¾ tsp. ground ancho chile pepper
- ½ tsp. salt
- ¼ tsp. crushed red pepper (optional)
- 3 Tbsp. butter

1. Preheat oven to 350°F. Arrange squash halves, cut sides up, in a 3-qt. rectangular baking dish.

2. In a small bowl stir together brown sugar, ancho pepper, salt, and, if desired, crushed red pepper. Divide brown sugar mixture and butter among squash halves.

3. Pour about ¼ inch water into the baking dish. Cover tightly with foil. Bake 1¼ hours or until squash is tender.

NUMBER OF SERVINGS 6

PER SERVING *159 cal., 6 g fat (4 g sat. fat), 15 mg chol., 247 mg sodium, 28 g carb., 2 g fiber, 12 g sugars, 1 g pro.*

SNICKEROONI BARS
Recipe on page 231

BARS BEYOND BROWNIES

COCONUT JOY CANDY BARS

PREP 20 minutes **BAKE** 32 minutes at 350°F **COOL** 30 minutes + 1 hour **CHILL** 1 hour

Nonstick cooking spray

¾ cup butter, melted

2 cups sugar

2 tsp. vanilla

3 eggs, lightly beaten

1¼ cups all-purpose flour

½ cup unsweetened cocoa powder

1 tsp. baking powder

½ tsp. salt

4 cups flaked coconut

1 14-oz. can sweetened condensed milk

½ tsp. almond extract

½ cup chopped almonds, toasted (tip, page 21)

1 recipe Milk Chocolate Ganache

1. Preheat oven to 350°F. Line a 13×9-inch baking pan with foil, extending foil over edges of pan. Lightly coat foil with cooking spray. In a large bowl stir together melted butter, sugar, and 1 tsp. of the vanilla until combined. Stir in eggs until combined.

2. In another bowl combine flour, cocoa powder, baking powder, and salt. Add flour mixture to butter mixture; stir until combined. Spread half the batter into the prepared pan. Bake 12 minutes or just until set. Cool in pan on a wire rack 30 minutes.

3. Meanwhile, for filling, in a large bowl combine coconut, condensed milk, the remaining 1 tsp. vanilla, and the almond extract.

4. Spread filling over baked chocolate layer; sprinkle with almonds. Carefully spread the remaining chocolate batter over filling. Bake 20 to 25 minutes or until chocolate layer is set. Cool completely on a wire rack, about 1 hour.

5. Spoon Milk Chocolate Ganache over cooled bars, spreading evenly. Chill at least 1 hour or until ganache is firm. Use foil to lift uncut bars out of pan; cut into bars.

NUMBER OF SERVINGS 48

MILK CHOCOLATE GANACHE Pour one 11.5-oz. pkg. milk chocolate pieces into a medium bowl. In a small saucepan bring ¾ cup heavy cream just to boiling. Immediately pour cream over chocolate in bowl. Let stand, without stirring, 5 minutes. Stir until smooth.

PER BAR *187 cal., 10 g fat (6 g sat. fat), 28 mg chol., 96 mg sodium, 24 g carb., 1 g fiber, 19 g sugars, 3 g pro.*

Place bars in a single layer in an airtight container. Store in the refrigerator up to 3 days or freeze up to 3 months.

CANDY-CRUNCH PEANUT BUTTER BARS

PREP 30 minutes   **CHILL** 1 hour

30 peanut butter sandwich
   cookies with peanut butter
   filling

¼ tsp. salt

½ cup butter, melted

2 cups powdered sugar

1⅓ cups creamy peanut butter

½ cup butter, softened

2 Tbsp. heavy cream

½ cup finely crushed peanuts
   with crunchy sugar coating
   (French burnt peanuts)
   or other candy-coated
   peanuts

1 cup semisweet chocolate
   pieces

½ cup creamy peanut butter

1. Line a 13×9-inch baking pan with foil, extending foil over edges of pan. For crust, in a food processor combine cookies and salt. Cover and process until finely ground. Add the melted butter. Cover and pulse just until combined. Press mixture into the prepared baking pan.

2. In a large bowl beat powdered sugar, the 1⅓ cups peanut butter, the softened butter, and cream on low to medium until smooth. Stir in peanuts. Carefully spread mixture over crust.

3. In a small heavy saucepan heat and stir chocolate pieces and the ½ cup peanut butter over low heat until melted. Spread mixture over layers in pan. Sprinkle with additional crushed peanuts.

4. Cover and chill about 1 hour or until set. Use foil to lift uncut bars out of pan; cut into bars.

NUMBER OF SERVINGS 48

PER BAR *182 cal., 12 g fat (5 g sat. fat), 11 mg chol., 127 mg sodium, 17 g carb., 1 g fiber, 11 g sugars, 4 g pro.*

Layer bars between sheets of waxed paper in an airtight container. Store in the refrigerator up to 1 week.

CHOCOLATY CARAMEL-NUT S'MORE BARS

PREP 30 minutes **BAKE** 27 minutes at 325°F

Skip the campfire and enjoy favorite flavors of summer with these s'mores-gone-wild bars—layers of chocolaty cookies, chewy caramel, fluffy marshmallows, and salty nuts.

2 cups finely crushed chocolate wafers (38 cookies)

½ cup butter, melted

1 11-oz. pkg. caramel baking bits*

¼ cup heavy cream*

2 cups tiny marshmallows

1½ cups mixed nuts, cashews, or cocktail peanuts, coarsely chopped

1 cup semisweet chocolate pieces

1. Preheat oven to 325°F. Line a 13×9-inch baking pan with foil, extending foil over edges of pan. Lightly grease foil.

2. In a bowl stir together the crushed cookies and butter. Press crumb mixture into bottom of prepared pan. Bake 15 minutes. Cool on a wire rack 5 minutes.

3. Meanwhile, in a small heavy saucepan heat and stir caramel bits and cream until melted and smooth. Pour evenly over crust.

4. Sprinkle marshmallows, nuts, and chocolate pieces over caramel mixture; press in lightly.

5. Bake about 12 minutes or just until marshmallows begin to brown. Cool in pan on a wire rack. Use foil to lift uncut bars out of pan; cut into bars.

NUMBER OF SERVINGS 24

*TIP If you can't find caramel baking bits, use one 14-oz. pkg. vanilla caramels and increase cream to ⅓ cup.

PER BAR *237 cal., 15 g fat (7 g sat. fat), 14 mg chol., 163 mg sodium, 27 g carb., 1 g fiber, 19 g sugars, 3 g pro.*

MAKE AHEAD

Layer bars between sheets of waxed paper in an airtight container. Store in the refrigerator up to 3 days or freeze up to 3 months.

SNICKEROONI BARS

PREP 30 minutes **BAKE** 12 minutes at 350°F **FREEZE** 30 minutes **CHILL** 2 hours

Nonstick cooking spray

1 14.3-oz. pkg. chocolate sandwich cookies with white filling (36 cookies)

⅓ cup butter, melted

1¼ cups sugar

⅓ cup butter, cut up

1 5-oz. can (⅔ cup) evaporated milk

1 7-oz. jar marshmallow creme

¼ cup creamy peanut butter

1¾ cups cocktail peanuts or salted cashews, chopped

1 14-oz. bag vanilla caramels (about 50), unwrapped

1½ cups milk chocolate pieces (8 oz.)

1. Preheat oven to 350°F. Line a 13×9-inch baking pan with foil, extending foil over edges of pan. Lightly coat foil with cooking spray. Place cookies in a food processor. Cover and process until very finely chopped. In a bowl combine cookie crumbs and ⅓ cup melted butter. Firmly press crumb mixture into the prepared pan. Bake 12 minutes or until set. Cool in pan on a wire rack.

2. For the nougat, in a medium saucepan combine sugar, ⅓ cup butter, and ½ cup of the evaporated milk. Bring to boiling over medium-high heat, stirring to dissolve sugar. Reduce heat to medium. Simmer, uncovered, 10 minutes. Remove saucepan from heat. Stir in marshmallow creme and peanut butter. Stir in chopped nuts. Pour nougat over crust, carefully spreading to edges. Place pan in freezer 20 minutes while preparing caramel layer.

3. For caramel layer, in a medium bowl place caramels and the remaining evaporated milk (about 2 Tbsp.). Microwave 1½ to 2 minutes or until caramels are melted, stirring every 30 seconds. Pour caramel mixture over nougat layer, carefully spreading to edges of pan. Return pan to freezer 10 to 15 minutes while preparing last layer.

4. In a small bowl microwave chocolate pieces for 1 minute or until melted and smooth, stirring every 30 seconds. Pour chocolate mixture over caramel layer, spreading to edges. Cover and chill 2 hours or until firm. Use edges of foil to lift uncut bars out of pan; cut into bars.

NUMBER OF SERVINGS 60

PER BAR *154 cal., 8 g fat (3 g sat. fat), 7 mg chol., 86 mg sodium, 20 g carb., 1 g fiber, 14 g sugars, 2 g pro.*

Layer bars between sheets of waxed paper in an airtight container. Store in the refrigerator up to 5 days or freeze up to 3 months.

FUDGY BROWNIES

PREP 15 minutes **BAKE** 35 minutes at 350°F

9 oz. unsweetened chocolate, coarsely chopped

1 cup butter, cut up

⅓ cup water

4 tsp. instant coffee crystals

1½ cups granulated sugar

1½ cups packed brown sugar

5 eggs

1½ tsp. vanilla

2 cups all-purpose flour

¾ cup ground almonds

½ tsp. ground cinnamon

¼ tsp. salt

1 recipe Bittersweet Ganache (optional)

1 recipe Chocolate Drizzle (optional)

1. Preheat oven to 350°F. For easy cleanup, line a 13×9-inch baking pan with foil, extending foil over edges of pan. Grease foil or pan.

2. In a large bowl combine chocolate, butter, the water, and coffee crystals. Microwave, uncovered, 2 to 4 minutes or until butter is melted, stirring once or twice. Remove from microwave. Stir until smooth.

3. Beat in sugars with a mixer on low to medium until combined. Add eggs and vanilla; beat on medium 2 minutes. Add flour, almonds, cinnamon, and salt; beat on low until combined. Spread batter in the prepared pan.

4. Bake 35 minutes or until top appears set and dry. Cool in pan on a wire rack. If desired, pour Bittersweet Ganache over brownies and, if desired, drizzle with Chocolate Drizzle. If using foil, lift uncut bars out of pan; cut into bars.

NUMBER OF SERVINGS 64

PER BAR *302 cal., 17 g fat (9 g sat. fat), 66 mg chol., 127 mg sodium, 37 g carb., 2 g fiber, 24 g sugars, 4 g pro.*

BITTERSWEET GANACHE In a medium saucepan bring 1 cup whipping cream just to boiling over medium-high heat. Remove from heat. Add 12 oz. bittersweet chocolate, chopped (do not stir). Let stand 5 minutes. Stir until smooth. Cool 15 minutes before using.

CHOCOLATE DRIZZLE In a small bowl combine 2 oz. chopped white baking chocolate, 2 oz. chopped milk chocolate, and 2 tsp. shortening. Microwave 2 minutes or until melted and smooth, stirring every 30 seconds. Drizzle melted chocolate over Bitterweet Ganache.

Place brownies in a single layer in an airtight container. Store in the refrigerator up to 3 days.

CHERRY-CABERNET BROWNIES

PREP 30 minutes **BAKE** 30 minutes at 350°F **STAND** 2 hours

- 1 cup dried cherries, chopped
- ½ cup Cabernet Sauvignon or other fruity red wine
- ¾ cup butter, cut up
- 4 oz. unsweetened chocolate, chopped
- 2 cups sugar
- 3 eggs
- 1 tsp. vanilla
- 1 cup all-purpose flour
- ½ tsp. baking powder
- ¼ tsp. baking soda
- ¼ tsp. salt
- 1 recipe Red Wine Ganache

1. In a small saucepan combine dried cherries and wine. Bring just to boiling; remove from heat. Preheat oven to 350°F. Line a 13×9-inch baking pan with foil, extending foil over edges of pan. Grease and lightly flour foil.

2. In a medium saucepan heat and stir butter and chocolate over low heat until melted. Gradually whisk in sugar until dissolved. Add eggs, one at a time, whisking well after each addition. Stir in vanilla. In a bowl stir together flour, baking powder, baking soda, and salt. Stir flour mixture into chocolate mixture until combined. Stir in undrained cherries. Spread batter in the prepared baking pan.

3. Bake 30 minutes or until edges start to pull away from sides of pan. Cool in pan on a wire rack.

4. Spread Red Wine Ganache over uncut brownies. Let stand 2 hours or until set. Use foil to lift uncut brownies out of pan; cut into bars.

NUMBER OF SERVINGS 36

RED WINE GANACHE In a small heavy saucepan combine 6 oz. chopped semisweet chocolate, 3 Tbsp. butter, and 3 Tbsp. Cabernet Sauvignon or other fruity red wine. Heat and stir over low heat until melted and smooth.

PER BAR *158 cal., 8 g fat (5 g sat. fat), 28 mg chol., 82 mg sodium, 21 g carb., 1 g fiber, 16 g sugars, 2 g pro.*

Place brownies in a single layer in an airtight container. Store at room temperature up to 3 days or freeze up to 3 months.

LEMONY GLAZED SHORTBREAD BARS

PREP 40 minutes **BAKE** 40 minutes at 300°F

Rubbing lemon zest into sugar is an important step and worth the effort. This simple technique releases oils from the zest for intense flavor and color.

3 cups all-purpose flour

⅓ cup cornstarch

5 to 6 lemons

1¼ cups powdered sugar

1½ cups butter, softened

½ tsp. salt

½ tsp. vanilla

1 recipe Lemony Glaze

1. Preheat oven to 300°F. Line a 13×9-inch baking pan with foil, extending foil over edges of pan. Lightly grease foil. In a bowl stir together flour and cornstarch.

2. Remove ¼ cup zest from the lemons and squeeze 1 Tbsp. juice from one the lemon. In a bowl combine powdered sugar and the lemon zest. Use a wooden spoon to press zest into powdered sugar against the side of bowl until sugar is yellow and very fragrant.

3. In a large bowl beat butter, the lemon juice, salt, and vanilla with a mixer on medium until combined. Gradually beat in sugar mixture. Stir in flour mixture. With lightly floured fingers, press dough evenly into the prepared pan.

4. Bake 40 minutes or until pale golden in color and edges start to brown.

5. Immediately spoon Lemony Glaze over hot bars and gently spread to edges. Cool in pan on a wire rack. Use foil to lift uncut bars out of the pan; cut into bars.

NUMBER OF SERVINGS 32

LEMONY GLAZE Remove 2 tsp. zest and squeeze 3 Tbsp. lemon juice from 1 or 2 lemons. In a bowl whisk together lemon zest and juice, 2½ cups powdered sugar, 1 Tbsp. light-color corn syrup, and ½ tsp. vanilla until smooth.

PER BAR *181 cal., 9 g fat (5 g sat. fat), 23 mg chol., 98 mg sodium, 25 g carb., 0 g fiber, 14 g sugars, 1 g pro.*

Layer bars between sheets of waxed paper in an airtight container. Store in the refrigerator up to 3 days or freeze up to 3 months.

TANGY APRICOT-ROSEMARY STREUSEL BARS

PREP 40 minutes **BAKE** 40 minutes at 350°F

3 cups all-purpose flour

1¾ cups granulated sugar

2 tsp. snipped fresh
   rosemary

1 tsp. baking powder

1¼ tsp. salt

1 cup butter, cut up

2 15-oz. cans unpeeled
   apricot halves in light syrup,
   undrained

⅓ cup cold water

2 Tbsp. cornstarch

2 Tbsp. butter

⅓ cup pine nuts

1 cup powdered sugar

¼ tsp. vanilla

1 to 2 Tbsp. milk

1. Preheat oven to 350°F. Line a 13×9-inch baking pan with foil, extending foil over edges of pan. Lightly grease foil.

2. For crust, in a large bowl stir together flour, 1 cup of the granulated sugar, the rosemary, baking powder, and 1 tsp. of the salt. Using a pastry blender, cut in the 1 cup butter until mixture resembles coarse crumbs. Remove 1½ cups of the crumb mixture for topping. Press the remaining mixture into the prepared baking pan. Bake 10 to 12 minutes or until set.

3. Meanwhile, drain apricots, reserving ¼ cup of the syrup. In a medium saucepan combine apricots, the reserved syrup, the remaining ¾ cup granulated sugar, the water, cornstarch, the 2 Tbsp. butter, and the remaining ¼ tsp. salt. Cook and stir over medium heat until thickened and bubbly. Cook and stir 1 minute more. Spoon apricot mixture evenly over hot crust. Combine the reserved crumb mixture and pine nuts; sprinkle over apricot mixture.

4. Bake 30 minutes or until filling is bubbly around the edges and topping is lightly browned. Cool in pan on a wire rack.

5. For icing, in a bowl stir together powdered sugar and vanilla. Stir in enough of the milk, 1 tsp. at a time, to make drizzling consistency. Drizzle icing over uncut bars; let stand until icing is set. Use foil to lift uncut bars out of pan; cut into bars.

NUMBER OF SERVINGS 32

PER BAR *181 cal., 7 g fat (4 g sat. fat), 17 mg chol., 165 mg sodium, 28 g carb., 1 g fiber, 18 g sugars, 2 g pro.*

Place bars in a single layer in an airtight container. Store in the refrigerator up to 3 days or freeze up to 3 months.

PISTACHIO-CRANBERRY BAKLAVA

PREP 45 minutes **BAKE** 35 minutes at 325°F **BAKE** 35 minutes at 325°F

1½ cups pistachio nuts, finely chopped

1½ cups dried cranberries

1⅓ cups sugar

½ tsp. ground cardamom

¾ cup butter, melted

½ 16-oz. pkg. (20 to 24 sheets) frozen phyllo dough (14×9-inch rectangles), thawed

¾ cup water

3 Tbsp. honey

1 tsp. vanilla

1. Preheat oven to 325°F. For filling, in a bowl stir together pistachio nuts, cranberries, ⅓ cup of the sugar, and the cardamom.

2. Brush the bottom of a 13×9-inch baking pan with some of the melted butter. Unroll phyllo dough; cover phyllo dough with plastic wrap. Layer one-fourth (5 or 6) of the phyllo dough sheets in the prepared baking pan, brushing each sheet generously with some of the melted butter. Sprinkle layers with about 1 cup of the filling. Repeat layering phyllo dough sheets and filling twice more, brushing each sheet with melted butter.

3. Layer the remaining phyllo dough sheets on top of the last layer of filling, brushing each sheet with melted butter. Drizzle with any remaining melted butter. Using a sharp knife, cut baklava into 24 to 48 diamond, rectangle, or square pieces.

4. Bake 35 to 45 minutes or until golden. Cool slightly in pan on a wire rack.

5. Meanwhile, for syrup, in a medium saucepan stir together the remaining 1 cup sugar, the water, honey, and vanilla. Bring to boiling; reduce heat. Simmer, uncovered, 20 minutes. Pour the syrup over the slightly cooled baklava; cool completely.

NUMBER OF SERVINGS 24

PER PIECE *200 cal., 10 g fat (4 g sat. fat), 15 mg chol., 131 mg sodium, 27 g carb., 1 g fiber, 19 g sugars, 2 g pro.*

PEANUT BAKLAVA Prepare Pistachio-Cranberry Baklava as directed, except substitute 3 cups finely chopped peanuts for the pistachio nuts and cranberries and substitute 1 tsp. ground cinnamon for the cardamom. Increase sugar to 1½ cups and use ½ cup of the sugar in Step 1. Continue as directed. For the syrup, add 2 inches stick cinnamon before boiling. Remove cinnamon before pouring syrup over baklava.

PER PIECE *243 cal., 15 g fat (5 g sat. fat), 15 mg chol., 98 mg sodium, 24 g carb., 2 g fiber, 16 g sugars, 5 g pro.*

MAKE AHEAD

Layer pieces between sheets of waxed paper in an airtight container. Store in the refrigerator up to 3 days or freeze up to 3 months.

**STONE FRUIT–
COCONUT CRISP**
Recipe on page 254

PAN PIES & BUBBLY BAKES

RASPBERRY FRENCH SILK PAN PIE

PREP 40 minutes **BAKE** 10 minutes at 375°F **CHILL** 2 hours

1 recipe Chocolate Crumb Crust

1 cup heavy cream

3 oz. semisweet chocolate, chopped

3 oz. bittersweet chocolate, chopped

⅓ cup sugar

⅓ cup butter

2 egg yolks, lightly beaten

3 Tbsp. crème de cacao or whipping cream

½ cup raspberry preserves or seedless raspberry jam

1 recipe Raspberry Ganache

Fresh raspberries (optional)

1. Preheat oven to 375°F. Line a 13×9-inch baking pan with foil, extending foil over edges of pan. Press Chocolate Crumb Crust onto the bottom and slightly up sides of the prepared pan. Bake 10 minutes or until crust is set. Cool in pan on a wire rack.

2. Meanwhile, for filling, in a medium-size heavy saucepan combine the next five ingredients (through butter). Heat and stir over low heat 10 minutes or until chocolate is melted and smooth. Remove from heat. Gradually stir half the hot mixture into the beaten egg yolks. Add egg yolk mixture to chocolate mixture in saucepan. Cook and stir over medium-low heat about 5 minutes or until slightly thickened and bubbly. Remove from heat. (Mixture may appear slightly curdled.) Stir in the crème de cacao. Place the saucepan in a bowl of ice water for 20 minutes or until filling thickens and becomes hard to stir, stirring occasionally. Transfer filling to a medium bowl; set aside.

3. Spread raspberry preserves over cooled Chocolate Crumb Crust. Beat filling with a mixer on medium to high 2 to 3 minutes or until light and fluffy. Spread filling over preserves. Cover and chill 1 to 2 hours or until firm.

4. Gently spread Raspberry Ganache over bars. Cover and chill 1 to 2 hours or until firm. Use foil to lift uncut pie out of pan. Cut into bars. If desired, top with fresh raspberries.

NUMBER OF SERVINGS 32

CHOCOLATE CRUMB CRUST In a bowl combine 2 cups finely crushed chocolate wafers, chocolate graham crackers, or other crisp chocolate cookies; ¼ cup all-purpose flour; and 2 Tbsp. granulated sugar. Stir in ¼ cup melted butter until combined.

RASPBERRY GANACHE In a 4-cup glass measuring cup combine 1 cup chopped semisweet chocolate or chocolate pieces, ⅓ cup heavy cream, and 1 Tbsp. seedless raspberry jam. Microwave 1 minute or until smooth, stirring every 30 seconds. Let stand 1 hour or until slightly thickened.

PER BAR *201 cal., 13 g fat (8 g sat. fat), 39 mg chol., 104 mg sodium, 21 g carb., 1 g fiber, 14 g sugars, 2 g pro.*

Place bars in a single layer in an airtight container. Store in the refrigerator up to 3 days.

DOUGHNUT-APPLE COBBLER

PREP 30 minutes **BAKE** 55 minutes at 375°F

10 medium baking apples, peeled, cored, and sliced

1 large lemon, juiced and pulp reserved

½ cup sugar

⅓ cup all-purpose flour

1 tsp. ground cinnamon

12 cinnamon-sugar-coated cake doughnuts

5 Tbsp. butter, melted

Vanilla ice cream (optional)

1. Preheat oven to 375°F. In a large bowl combine apple slices, lemon juice, and any lemon pulp. Sprinkle with sugar, flour, and cinnamon; toss until apples are coated. Arrange apples in a 3-qt. rectangular baking dish.

2. Bake, covered, 40 minutes or until apples are tender. Uncover; top apples with doughnuts, squeezing to fit if necessary, and drizzle with melted butter. Bake, uncovered, 15 minutes or until hot and bubbly. If desired, serve warm with ice cream.

NUMBER OF SERVINGS 12

PER SERVING *359 cal., 15 g fat (6 g sat. fat), 27 mg chol., 221 mg sodium, 55 g carb., 5 g fiber, 24 g sugars, 3 g pro.*

BLACKBERRY-BLUEBERRY COBBLER SUPREME

PREP 25 minutes   **BAKE** 40 minutes at 350°F   **COOL** 30 minutes

If fresh berries aren't in season, make this cakelike cobbler with thawed frozen blackberries and blueberries. Drain fruit, reserving juice. then add enough water to juice to equal 1½ cups to substitute for the water in the recipe.

1 cup all-purpose flour

1 cup whole wheat flour

2 tsp. baking powder

¼ tsp. salt

½ cup butter, softened

1 cup granulated sugar

¾ cup milk

3 cups fresh blackberries

1½ cups fresh blueberries

½ cup granulated sugar

1½ cups water

Powdered sugar (optional)

Ice cream or half-and-half (optional)

1. Preheat oven to 350°F. Grease a 3-qt. rectangular baking dish. In a bowl stir together the flours, baking powder, and salt.

2. In a large bowl beat butter with a mixer on medium to high 30 seconds. Beat in the 1 cup granulated sugar until fluffy. Alternately add flour mixture and milk to butter mixture, beating on low after each addition just until combined.

3. Spread batter in the prepared baking dish. Top with blackberries and blueberries; sprinkle with the ½ cup granulated sugar. Pour the water over fruit.

4. Bake 40 to 50 minutes or until a toothpick inserted in the cake comes out clean. (Some fruit will sink as the cobbler rises.) Cool on a wire rack 30 minutes. Serve warm. If desired, sprinkle lightly with powdered sugar and serve with ice cream.

NUMBER OF SERVINGS 12

PER SERVING *271 cal., 9 g fat (5 g sat. fat), 22 mg chol., 206 mg sodium, 47 g carb., 4 g fiber, 30 g sugars, 4 g pro.*

STONE FRUIT-COCONUT CRISP

PREP 40 minutes **BAKE** 25 minutes at 375°F

This is the recipe to make when stone fruits are in peak season—when they're best for flavor and juiciness. If you crave this crisp when fresh stone fruit is out of season, use frozen unsweetened peach slices, thawed.

4 cups fresh or frozen pitted Royal Ann or dark sweet cherries

1 to 2 oranges

½ cup granulated sugar

3 Tbsp. cornstarch

6 cups sliced stone fruit, such as nectarines, plums, and/or peeled peaches

¾ cup rolled oats

½ cup packed brown sugar

⅓ cup all-purpose flour

⅓ cup butter, cut up

1 cup flaked coconut

Coconut or vanilla ice cream (optional)

1. If using frozen cherries, let stand at room temperature 30 minutes (do not drain). Preheat oven to 375°F. Remove 1 Tbsp. zest and squeeze ½ cup juice from oranges. In a 4- to 6- qt. Dutch oven stir together granulated sugar and cornstarch. Stir in cherries, stone fruit, and orange juice. Cook and stir over medium heat until thickened and bubbly. Transfer to a 3-qt. rectangular baking dish.

2. For topping, in a bowl stir together oats, brown sugar, flour, and orange zest. Using a pastry blender, cut in butter until mixture resembles coarse crumbs. Stir in coconut. Sprinkle topping over fruit mixture.

3. Bake 25 minutes or until stone fruit is tender and topping is golden. Serve warm and, if desired, with ice cream.

NUMBER OF SERVINGS 8

PER SERVING *420 cal., 13 g fat (9 g sat. fat), 20 mg chol., 103 mg sodium, 74 g carb., 6 g fiber, 53 g sugars, 5 g pro.*

GINGERED CHERRY COBBLER

PREP 25 minutes   **BAKE** 20 minutes at 400°F   **COOL** 30 minutes

1½ cups all-purpose flour*

½ cup packed brown sugar

½ cup rolled oats

2 tsp. baking powder

½ tsp. salt

½ tsp. baking soda

½ cup butter, cut up

8 cups fresh or frozen unsweetened pitted tart red cherries

¾ cup granulated sugar

¼ cup chopped crystallized ginger

3 Tbsp. cornstarch

½ tsp. ground cinnamon

1 egg, lightly beaten

¾ cup milk

½ cup pecan pieces or chopped almonds (optional)

1 Tbsp. coarse white decorating sugar

Whipped cream (optional)

1. Preheat oven to 400°F. Grease a 3-qt. rectangular baking dish. For topping, in a bowl stir together the first six ingredients (through baking soda). Using a pastry blender, cut in butter until mixture resembles coarse crumbs.

2. For filling, in a large saucepan combine the next five ingredients (through cinnamon). Cook over medium heat until cherries release their juice, stirring occasionally. Continue to cook, stirring constantly, over medium heat until thickened and bubbly. Keep filling hot.

3. In a bowl stir together egg and milk. Add to flour mixture, stirring just until moistened. Pour hot cherry filling into baking dish. Immediately drop dough into 10 to 12 mounds on top of hot filling. Sprinkle dough with nuts, if desired, and coarse sugar.

4. Bake, uncovered, 20 to 25 minutes or until topping is golden brown and a toothpick inserted in topping comes out clean. Cool in dish on a wire rack 30 minutes. If desired, serve warm with whipped cream.

NUMBER OF SERVINGS 8

***TIP** If desired, use 1 cup all-purpose flour and ½ cup whole wheat flour.

PER SERVING *484 cal., 14 g fat (8 g sat. fat), 59 mg chol., 397 mg sodium, 86 g carb., 4 g fiber, 48 g sugars, 7 g pro.*

PEACH PINWHEEL DUMPLINGS

PREP 45 minutes **BAKE** 45 minutes at 350°F **COOL** 30 minutes

½ cup butter

2 cups sugar

2 cups water

1 tsp. vanilla

2 cups self-rising flour

½ cup shortening

½ cup milk

5 cups chopped, pitted and peeled peaches or frozen unsweetened peach slices, thawed and chopped

½ tsp. ground cinnamon

¼ to ½ tsp. ground nutmeg

Vanilla ice cream

1. Preheat oven to 350°F. Place butter in a 3-qt. rectangular baking dish. Set in oven 5 to 8 minutes or until butter is melted. Remove dish from oven; set aside.

2. For syrup, in a medium saucepan combine sugar and the water. Cook and stir over medium heat until sugar is dissolved. Bring to boiling; boil, uncovered, 5 minutes. Remove from heat; stir in vanilla. Cover and keep warm.

3. For dough, place flour in a large bowl. Using a pastry blender, cut in shortening until pieces are pea-size. Make a well in center. Add milk all at once. Stir just until moistened. Knead dough on a lightly floured 14×12-inch piece of waxed paper 10 to 12 strokes or until nearly smooth. Lightly sprinkle dough with additional flour. Cover with another 14×12-inch piece of waxed paper. Roll out dough to a 12×10-inch rectangle (about ¼ inch thick).

4. For filling, in another large bowl combine peaches, cinnamon, and nutmeg. Spoon 3 cups of the peaches over butter in baking dish. Spoon the remaining 2 cups peaches over the dough rectangle. Starting from a long edge, roll dough into a spiral,. Pinch seam to seal. Cut into 12 slices. Arrange rolls, cut sides down, over the peaches. Pour syrup carefully around rolls. (This will look like too much syrup, but the rolls will absorb the syrup during baking.)

5. Bake 45 to 50 minutes or until golden. Cool in pan on a wire rack 30 minutes. Serve warm with ice cream.

NUMBER OF SERVINGS 12

PER SERVING *453 cal., 21 g fat (10 g sat. fat), 37 mg chol., 345 mg sodium, 64 g carb., 2 g fiber, 47 g sugars, 4 g pro.*

BANANAS FOSTER BAKE

PREP 20 minutes **BAKE** 25 minutes at 375°F **COOL** 30 minutes

This classic rich combo eats like bread pudding. Get the best flavor by using dark rum and perfectly ripe bananas.

1 cup all-purpose flour

1 cup granulated sugar

1½ tsp. baking powder

½ tsp. salt

½ cup butter, melted

½ cup milk

¼ cup dark rum or milk

1 tsp. vanilla

4 medium bananas, peeled and sliced

½ cup raisins

1 cup rolled oats

¾ cup packed brown sugar

½ cup all-purpose flour

½ cup butter, cut up

½ cup chopped walnuts, pecans, or macadamia nuts

Vanilla bean ice cream (optional)

1. Preheat oven to 375°F. Grease a 3-qt. rectangular baking dish.

2. In a bowl stir together the first four ingredients (through salt); add melted butter, milk, rum, and vanilla. Stir until smooth. Spread batter in the prepared baking dish. Top with sliced bananas and raisins.

3. In a large bowl combine oats, brown sugar, and the ½ cup flour. Using a pastry blender, cut in the ½ cup butter until mixture resembles coarse crumbs. Stir in nuts. Sprinkle crumb mixture over batter.

4. Bake 25 to 30 minutes or until browned and set. Cool in pan on a wire rack 30 minutes. If desired, serve warm with ice cream.

NUMBER OF SERVINGS 12

PER SERVING *437 cal., 20 g fat (10 g sat. fat), 42 mg chol., 290 mg sodium, 62 g carb., 3 g fiber, 39 g sugars, 4 g pro.*

BANANA SPLIT CAKE
Recipe on page 275

CAKES TO TAKE

BLUEBERRY-LEMONADE POKE CAKE

PREP 20 minutes   **BAKE** 25 minutes at 350°F   **COOL** 2 hours

1 pkg. 2-layer-size white cake mix

1 cup buttermilk

4 eggs

⅓ cup canola oil

1 Tbsp. lemon zest

½ tsp. almond extract

1 recipe Blueberry Sauce

½ cup frozen lemonade concentrate, thawed

1 8-oz. container frozen whipped dessert topping, thawed

½ cup lemon curd

Quartered lemon slices (optional)

1. Preheat oven to 350°F. Grease a 13×9-inch baking pan.

2. In a large bowl combine the first six ingredients (through almond extract). Beat with a mixer on low just until combined. Beat on medium 2 minutes, scraping bowl occasionally. Spread batter into the prepared baking pan.

3. Bake 25 to 30 minutes or until a toothpick comes out clean. Meanwhile, prepare Blueberry Sauce. Cool cake 5 minutes.

4. Using the handle of a wooden spoon, poke holes through cake about 1 inch apart. Drizzle lemonade concentrate over top of cake, brushing evenly. Spread Blueberry Sauce over cake. Cool completely.

5. In a large bowl stir a small amount of the whipped topping into the lemon curd to lighten. Fold in the remaining whipped topping. Spread over cake. If desired, top servings with a lemon slice. Cover and store leftovers in the refrigerator up to 24 hours.

NUMBER OF SERVINGS 24

BLUEBERRY SAUCE In a medium saucepan combine ⅓ cup sugar and 1 tsp. cornstarch. Add ¼ cup water; mix well. Add 2 cups fresh or frozen blueberries. Cook and stir over medium heat until sauce is slightly thickened and bubbly. Cook and stir 2 minutes more. Mash with a potato masher (sauce will not be completely smooth).

PER SERVING *207 cal., 7 g fat (3 g sat. fat), 37 mg chol., 173 mg sodium, 32 g carb., 1 g fiber, 22 g sugars, 3 g pro.*

GOOEY CHOCOLATE-CARAMEL CAKE

PREP 15 minutes **BAKE** according to package directions **COOL** 2 hours

1 pkg. 2-layer-size German chocolate cake mix

1 14-oz. can sweetened condensed milk

1 12-oz. jar caramel-flavor ice cream topping

1 8-oz. container frozen whipped dessert topping, thawed

3 1.4-oz. bars chocolate-covered English toffee, chopped

1. Preheat oven to 350°F. Grease and lightly flour a 13×9-inch baking pan.

2. Prepare cake mix according to package directions. Pour into prepared pan. Bake according to package directions. Cool cake in pan on a wire rack.

3. Using the handle of a wooden spoon, poke holes into cake about 1 inch apart. Slowly pour sweetened condensed milk over cake, then slowly pour caramel topping over cake. Spread evenly with dessert topping. Before serving, sprinkle with chopped toffee.

NUMBER OF SERVINGS 30

PER SERVING 186 cal., 5 g fat (3 g sat. fat), 6 mg chol., 197 mg sodium, 33 g carb., 1 g fiber, 25 g sugars, 2 g pro.

Prepare as directed, except do not sprinkle with chopped toffee. Cover and store cake in the refrigerator up to 24 hours. Before serving, sprinkle with chopped toffee.

BUTTERSCOTCH MARBLE CAKE

PREP 25 minutes **BAKE** 30 minutes at 350°F **COOL** 2 hours

1 pkg. 2-layer-size white cake mix

1 pkg. 4-serving-size butterscotch instant pudding and pie filling mix

1 cup water

4 eggs

¼ cup vegetable oil

½ cup chocolate-flavor syrup

3 oz. sweet baking chocolate, chopped

3 Tbsp. butter

1 cup powdered sugar

2 Tbsp. hot water

1. Preheat oven to 350°F. Grease and flour a 13×9-inch baking pan.

2. In a bowl combine the first five ingredients (through oil). Beat with a mixer on low just until combined. Beat on medium 2 minutes, scraping bowl occasionally.

3. Transfer 1½ cups of the batter to another bowl; stir in chocolate syrup. Spread light-color batter into the prepared pan. Top with spoonfuls of the chocolate batter. Using a table knife or thin metal spatula, gently cut through batters to swirl them together.

4. Bake 30 to 35 minutes or until a toothpick comes out clean. Cool in pan on a wire rack.

5. For icing, in a small saucepan combine sweet baking chocolate and the butter. Heat and stir over low heat until melted. Remove from heat. Stir in powdered sugar and the hot water. If necessary, stir in additional hot water, 1 tsp. at a time, until icing reaches drizzling consistency. Drizzle icing over cake.

NUMBER OF SERVINGS 16

PER SERVING 290 cal., 10 g fat (4 g sat. fat), 52 mg chol., 366 mg sodium, 49 g carb., 1 g fiber, 34 g sugars, 4 g pro.

MAKE AHEAD

Cover and store iced cake at room temperature up to 3 days. Or do not frost cake; cover and freeze up to 4 months. Thaw frozen cake at room temperature before icing.

DARK COCOA BUTTERMILK CAKE

PREP 35 minutes **BAKE** 45 minutes at 350°F **COOL** 2 hours

Dutch-process cocoa is not the average cocoa powder. It is made when regular cocoa powder is treated to neutralize its natural acidity, making it darker with a more mellow chocolaty flavor.

2⅓ cups all-purpose flour

¾ cup unsweetened dark Dutch-process cocoa powder or unsweetened cocoa powder

1 tsp. baking soda

¾ tsp. baking powder

½ tsp. salt

¾ cup butter, softened

1 cup granulated sugar

1 cup packed brown sugar

3 eggs, room temperature

2 tsp. vanilla

1½ cups buttermilk or sour milk*

1 recipe Cocoa Mascarpone Frosting

1. Preheat oven to 350°F. Lightly grease and flour a 13×9-inch baking pan. In a bowl stir together the first five ingredients (through salt).

2. In a large bowl beat butter with a mixer on medium 30 seconds. In another bowl combine sugars. Gradually add sugars to butter, ¼ cup at a time, beating on medium until combined. Scrape bowl; beat 2 minutes more. Add eggs, one at a time, beating after each addition. Beat in vanilla. Alternately add flour mixture and buttermilk, beating on low after each addition just until combined. Beat on medium 20 seconds more. Spread batter into prepared pan.

3. Bake 45 to 50 minutes or until a toothpick comes out clean. Cool cake in pan on a wire rack.

4. Spread cake with Cocoa Mascarpone Frosting. If desired, sprinkle with additional cocoa powder.

NUMBER OF SERVINGS 16

*TIP To make 1½ cups sour milk, place 4 tsp. lemon juice or vinegar in a glass measuring cup. Add enough milk to equal 1½ cups; stir. Let stand 5 minutes.

COCOA MASCARPONE FROSTING In a large bowl beat 2 oz. softened mascarpone or cream cheese, ¼ cup softened butter, 3 Tbsp. unsweetened dark Dutch-process cocoa powder or unsweetened cocoa powder, 1 Tbsp. milk, and 1 tsp. vanilla with a mixer on medium until creamy. Gradually add 2 to 2¼ cups powdered sugar, beating until smooth. Beat in additional milk, 1 tsp. at a time, to make spreading consistency.

PER SERVING *475 cal., 20 g fat (12 g sat. fat), 88 mg chol., 314 mg sodium, 74 g carb., 2 g fiber, 56 g sugars, 7 g pro.*

Cover and store frosted cake in the refrigerator up to 3 days. Or do not frost cake; cover and freeze up to 4 months. Thaw frozen cake at room temperature before frosting.

CHOCOLATE CHIP COOKIE CAKE

PREP 45 minutes **BAKE** 35 minutes at 375°F **COOL** 2 hours

Save some time: Instead of making the cake from scratch, use a 2-layer-size yellow or white cake mix and prepare according to package directions, except stir ¾ cup semisweet chocolate pieces into the batter. Layer and bake as directed.

2½ cups all-purpose flour

2½ tsp. baking powder

½ tsp. salt

¾ cup butter, softened

1¾ cups sugar

3 eggs

1½ tsp. vanilla

1¼ cups milk

¾ cup semisweet chocolate pieces

1 16.5- to 18-oz. pkg. refrigerated chocolate chip cookie dough

1 recipe Chocolate Butter Frosting

1. Preheat oven to 375°F. Grease and lightly flour a 13×9-inch baking pan. In a bowl stir together flour, baking powder, and salt.

2. In a large bowl beat butter with a mixer on medium 30 seconds. Gradually add sugar, about ¼ cup at a time, beating on medium until well combined. Scrape sides of bowl; beat 2 minutes more. Add eggs, one at a time, beating well after each addition. Beat in vanilla. Add flour mixture and milk alternately, beating on low after each addition just until combined. Stir in chocolate pieces. Spread half the batter into the prepared pan. Crumble half the cookie dough over batter. Repeat with remaining batter and cookie dough.

3. Bake 35 minutes or until a toothpick comes out clean (avoid cookie dough pieces). If needed, cover cake with foil the last 10 to 15 minutes of baking to prevent overbrowning. Cool in pan on a wire rack. Spread with Chocolate Butter Frosting.

NUMBER OF SERVINGS 16

CHOCOLATE BUTTER FROSTING In a large bowl beat 6 Tbsp. softened butter with a mixer on medium until smooth. Gradually beat in 1 cup powdered sugar. Beat in 2 Tbsp. milk and 1 tsp. vanilla. Gradually beat in an additional 2¾ cups powdered sugar and ¼ cup unsweetened cocoa powder. Beat in enough additional milk, 1 tsp. at a time, to reach spreading consistency.

PER SERVING *580 cal., 23 g fat (13 g sat. fat), 73 mg chol., 371 mg sodium, 90 g carb., 2 g fiber, 66 g sugars, 6 g pro.*

MAKE AHEAD

Cover and store frosted cake at room temperature up to 3 days. Or don't frost cake; cover and freeze up to 4 months. Thaw frozen cake at room temperature before frosting.

SPICE CAKE WITH COOKED COCONUT FROSTING

PREP 30 minutes **BAKE** 25 minutes at 350°F **COOL** 2 hours

The sweet and buttery flavor of gooey coconut frosting complements this moist nutmeg-infused cake. If you don't have a nutmeg grater, use a microplane grater or scrape the whole nutmeg with the edge of a paring knife.

2⅔ cups all-purpose flour

⅔ cup granulated sugar

⅔ cup packed brown sugar

1 Tbsp. baking powder

1 tsp. baking soda

1 tsp. grated whole nutmeg or ½ tsp. ground nutmeg

1⅓ cups milk

½ cup butter, softened

2 eggs, room temperature

2 tsp. vanilla

6 Tbsp. butter

1 cup flaked coconut

⅔ cup packed brown sugar

2 Tbsp. milk

⅔ cup chopped walnuts, toasted

1. Preheat oven to 350°F. Grease and flour a 13×9-inch baking pan.

2. In a large bowl combine the first six ingredients (through nutmeg). Add the next four ingredients (through vanilla). Beat with a mixer on low until combined. Beat on medium 1 minute. Pour batter into the prepared pan.

3. Bake 25 to 30 minutes or until a toothpick comes out clean.

4. Meanwhile, in a small saucepan combine the 6 Tbsp. butter, the coconut, ⅔ cup brown sugar, and the 2 Tbsp. milk. Cook and stir over medium heat until thickened and bubbly. Stir in walnuts. Spoon over hot cake. Cool cake in pan on a wire rack.

NUMBER OF SERVINGS 16

PER SERVING *343 cal., 16 g fat (8 g sat. fat), 52 mg chol., 288 mg sodium, 47 g carb., 1 g fiber, 29 g sugars, 5 g pro.*

PRALINE CRUNCH CAKE

PREP 30 minutes **BAKE** 40 minutes at 350°F **COOL** 2 hours

2 Tbsp. molasses

Water

1 Tbsp. instant coffee crystals

1 pkg. 2-layer-size yellow cake mix

3 eggs

⅓ cup vegetable oil

⅓ cup all-purpose flour

1 Tbsp. packed brown sugar

½ tsp. ground cinnamon

3 Tbsp. butter, cut up

⅓ cup coarsely chopped pecans

1 recipe Coffee Frosting

1. Preheat oven to 350°F. Grease a 13×9-inch baking pan.

2. Place molasses in a 2-cup glass measuring cup. Add enough water to equal 1⅓ cups; stir to combine. Pour liquid into a large bowl. Stir in coffee crystals until dissolved. Add cake mix, eggs, and oil. Beat with a mixer on low until combined. Beat on medium 2 minutes. Spread batter into the prepared baking pan.

3. Bake 30 minutes or until a toothpick comes out clean. Cool in pan on wire rack.

4. Meanwhile, for praline topping, in a bowl stir together flour, brown sugar, and cinnamon. Using a pastry blender, cut in butter until crumbly. Stir in pecans. Knead until mixture begins to form small moist clumps. Spread in an ungreased 15×10-inch baking pan. Bake 10 minutes or until lightly browned. Spread topping on a piece of foil; let cool.

5. Spread cooled cake with Coffee Frosting; sprinkle with praline topping.

NUMBER OF SERVINGS 16

COFFEE FROSTING In a bowl beat ⅓ cup softened butter with a mixer on low 30 seconds. Beat in 1 cup powdered sugar. In another bowl stir 1 tsp. coffee crystals into ⅓ cup half-and-half or milk until dissolved. Add coffee mixture and 1 tsp. vanilla to butter mixture; beat until combined (mixture may appear curdled). Gradually beat in 2½ cups powdered sugar until smooth. If necessary, beat in additional half-and-half, 1 tsp. at a time, to make frosting spreading consistency.

PER SERVING *381 cal., 16 g fat (6 g sat. fat), 53 mg chol., 277 mg sodium, 57 g carb., 0 g fiber, 42 g sugars, 3 g pro.*

MAKE AHEAD

Prepare as directed, except do not sprinkle with praline topping. Cover and store frosted cake at room temperature up to 3 days. Place praline mixture in an airtight container; cover and store at room temperature up to 3 days. Before serving, sprinkle cake with praline topping.

BANANA SPLIT CAKE

PREP 40 minutes **BAKE** 40 minutes at 350°F **COOL** 2 hours

Turn your favorite sundae into a marbled cake! Adding red food coloring to the strawberry swirl gives it a more striking contrast to the plain and chocolate batters.

3 cups all-purpose flour

2 tsp. baking powder

1 tsp. salt

¼ tsp. baking soda

1 cup butter, softened

1½ cups sugar

4 eggs, room temperature

½ cup mashed ripe banana (1 large)

½ cup sour cream

½ cup milk

1 tsp. vanilla

½ cup strawberry preserves

Few drops red food coloring

½ cup presweetened cocoa powder (not low-calorie)

1 cup chocolate fudge ice cream topping

Fresh strawberries (optional)

1. Preheat oven to 350°F. Grease and flour a 13×9-inch baking pan. In a bowl stir together flour, baking powder, salt, and baking soda.

2. In a large bowl beat butter with a mixer on medium to high 30 seconds. Gradually add sugar, ¼ cup at a time, beating until well combined and scraping sides of bowl occasionally. Add eggs, one at a time, beating until combined after each addition. In a small bowl combine banana, sour cream, milk, and vanilla. Alternately add flour mixture and banana mixture to butter mixture, beating on low after each addition just until combined.

3. In another bowl stir together 1 cup of the batter, the strawberry preserves, and red food coloring. In another bowl stir together another 1 cup of the batter and the cocoa powder. Spread the remaining plain batter into the prepared pan. Randomly spoon chocolate and strawberry batters in small mounds over the plain batter. Use a table knife or thin metal spatula to gently swirl the batters.

4. Bake 40 to 45 minutes or until a toothpick comes out clean. Cool completely in pan on a wire rack.

5. When ready to serve, in a small saucepan heat ice cream topping just until drizzling consistency. Cut cake into 16 pieces. Drizzle topping over cake. If desired, top each piece with a strawberry.

NUMBER OF SERVINGS 16

PER SERVING *414 cal., 17 g fat (9 g sat. fat), 81 mg chol., 382 mg sodium, 61 g carb., 1 g fiber, 34 g sugars, 6 g pro.*

MAKE AHEAD

Do not drizzle cooled cake with ice cream topping. Cover and store cake at room temperature up to 3 days or freeze up to 4 months. Thaw frozen cake at room temperature before drizzling with topping.

FRESH APPLE SNACK CAKE

PREP 30 minutes **BAKE** 50 minutes at 350°F **COOL** 1 hour

Here is a go-to cake when you need dessert for a crowd and have little time to prepare. Save even more time by leaving apples unpeeled (but scrub them well).

3 cups all-purpose flour

2 cups sugar

1 tsp. baking soda

1 tsp. salt

1 tsp. ground cinnamon

2 eggs, lightly beaten

1¼ cups canola oil or vegetable oil

2 tsp. vanilla

3 cups chopped, peeled Granny Smith apples

1 cup chopped pecans or walnuts, toasted (tip, page 21)

Whipped cream (optional)

1. Preheat oven to 350°F. Grease a 13×9-inch baking pan. In an extra-large bowl combine the first five ingredients (through cinnamon). Make a well in center of flour mixture.

2. In another bowl combine eggs, oil, and vanilla. Stir in apples and nuts. Add egg mixture to flour mixture, stirring just until moistened (batter will be thick). Spread batter into prepared pan.

3. Bake 50 to 55 minutes or until a toothpick comes out clean. Cool in pan on a wire rack 1 hour and serve slightly warm, or cool completely. If desired, serve with whipped cream.

NUMBER OF SERVINGS 20

PER SERVING *324 cal., 18 g fat (2 g sat. fat), 21 mg chol., 187 mg sodium, 38 g carb., 2 g fiber, 23 g sugars, 3 g pro.*

CARAMEL-FROSTED HUMMINGBIRD CAKE

PREP 30 minutes **BAKE** 40 minutes at 350°F **COOL** 2 hours

3 cups all-purpose flour

2 cups sugar

2 tsp. baking powder

1 tsp. salt

½ tsp. baking soda

½ tsp. ground cinnamon

2 cups mashed ripe bananas

1 8-oz. can crushed pineapple (juice pack)

1 cup vegetable oil

3 eggs, lightly beaten

½ cup flaked coconut

1½ tsp. vanilla

1 recipe Salty Caramel Cream Cheese Frosting

1. Preheat oven to 350°F. Lightly grease and flour a 13×9-inch baking pan.

2. In an extra-large bowl stir together the first six ingredients (through cinnamon). Add the next six ingredients (through vanilla), stirring just until combined. Spread batter into the prepared pan.

3. Bake 40 to 45 minutes or until a toothpick comes out clean. Cool cake in pan on a wire rack. Spread with Salty Caramel Cream Cheese Frosting.

NUMBER OF SERVINGS 16

SALTY CARAMEL CREAM CHEESE FROSTING In a bowl beat 4 oz. cream cheese, softened; ¼ cup butter, softened; ¼ cup caramel-flavor ice cream topping; 1 tsp. vanilla; and ¼ tsp. salt on medium until light and fluffy. Gradually beat in 2¾ to 3 cups powdered sugar to reach spreading consistency.

PER SERVING *513 cal., 21 g fat (6 g sat. fat), 50 mg chol., 371 mg sodium, 79 g carb., 1 g fiber, 57 g sugars, 5 g pro.*

MAKE AHEAD

Cover and store frosted cake in the refrigerator up to 3 days. Or don't frost cake; cover and freeze up to 4 months. Thaw frozen cake at room temperature before frosting.

GREEN APPLE-CHARDONNAY GRANITA
Recipe on page 294

14

FROZEN

FROSTY S'MORES

PREP 35 minutes **BAKE** 10 minutes at 350°F **FREEZE** 1 hour + overnight **BROIL** 30 seconds

Work quickly when topping the dessert with marshmallow creme and marshmallows. It should be as cold as possible before going under the broiler. If you have a culinary torch, use that for quick, controlled toasting.

15 graham cracker squares

1 cup sliced almonds

2 Tbsp. sugar

6 Tbsp. butter, melted

1 qt. (4 cups) chocolate-almond or chocolate ice cream

1 cup chocolate fudge-flavor ice cream topping

1 qt. (4 cups) salted caramel or vanilla ice cream

1 13-oz. jar marshmallow creme

3 cups tiny marshmallows

1 cup miniature semisweet chocolate pieces

1. Preheat oven to 350°F. For crust, in a food processor combine graham crackers, almonds, and sugar. Cover and pulse until crackers are finely crushed. Add melted butter; cover and pulse until crumbs are moistened. Press mixture into the bottom of a 13×9-inch baking pan. Bake 10 to 12 minutes or until edges start to brown. Cool on a wire rack.

2. Place chocolate-almond ice cream in a large bowl and stir until softened and spreadable. Spread over graham cracker layer. Swirl fudge topping over chocolate-almond ice cream. Freeze 1 hour or until ice cream is starting to firm.

3. Place salted caramel ice cream in a large bowl and stir until softened and spreadable. Spread salted caramel ice cream over chocolate and fudge layer. Cover and freeze overnight.

4. Preheat broiler. Quickly spread marshmallow creme over salted caramel ice cream layer. Sprinkle with marshmallows and chocolate pieces.

5. Broil 4 inches from the heat 30 to 60 seconds or just until marshmallows are golden. Cut dessert into squares. Serve immediately. Cover and freeze to store.

NUMBER OF SERVINGS 16

PER SQUARE *687 cal., 28 g fat (13 g sat. fat), 80 mg chol., 251 mg sodium, 105 g carb., 3 g fiber, 82 g sugars, 9 g pro.*

Prepare as directed through Step 3. Cover with plastic wrap, then with heavy foil. Freeze up to 1 month. To serve, continue as directed in Step 4.

BUTTERSCOTCH CRUNCH SQUARES

PREP 25 minutes **BAKE** 10 minutes at 400°F **FREEZE** 6 hours **STAND** 5 minutes

1 cup all-purpose flour

¼ cup quick-cooking rolled oats

¼ cup packed brown sugar

½ cup butter, cut up

½ cup chopped pecans or walnuts

½ cup butterscotch-flavor ice cream topping

½ gal. butter brickle or vanilla ice cream

1. Preheat oven to 400°F. In a bowl stir together flour, oats, and brown sugar. Using a pastry blender, cut in butter until mixture resembles coarse crumbs. Stir in nuts. Press mixture lightly into a 13×9-inch baking pan. Bake 10 to 15 minutes or until golden. While still warm, stir nut mixture to crumble; cool.

2. Spread half the crumbs in a 9-inch square baking pan; drizzle with half the butterscotch topping. Place ice cream in a bowl; stir to soften. Carefully spread ice cream over crumbs in pan. Top with the remaining butterscotch topping and crumbs.

3. Cover and freeze 6 hours or until firm. Let stand at room temperature 5 to 10 minutes before serving.

NUMBER OF SERVINGS 12

PER SQUARE *404 cal., 25 g fat (11 g sat. fat), 47 mg chol., 239 mg sodium, 43 g carb., 1 g fiber, 31 g sugars, 4 g pro.*

Prepare as directed through Step 1. Transfer crumb mixture to an airtight container; cover. Freeze up to 3 months.

LEMON BAR COOKIE ICE CREAM SANDWICHES

PREP 55 minutes   **BAKE** 10 minutes at 350°F   **COOL** 10 minutes   **FREEZE** 4 hours

¾ cup butter, softened

1½ cups sugar

4 tsp. lemon zest

¾ tsp. baking soda

¾ tsp. cream of tartar

½ tsp. salt

1 egg

1 egg yolk

1 tsp. vanilla

2¼ cups all-purpose flour

1½ qt. vanilla ice cream

1½ cups purchased lemon curd
(about two 10-oz. jars)

1 Tbsp. lemon zest

Crushed lemon drops
(optional)

1. Preheat oven to 350°F. Line a 13×9-inch baking pan with foil, extending foil over edges of pan. In a large bowl beat butter with a mixer on medium to high for 30 seconds. Add the next five ingredients (through salt). Beat until combined, scraping sides of bowl occasionally. Beat in egg, egg yolk, and vanilla until combined. Beat in as much of the flour as you can with the mixer. Stir in any remaining flour.

2. Press half of the dough into bottom of the prepared baking pan. Bake 10 to 12 minutes or until lightly browned. Cool in pan on a wire rack 5 minutes. Use foil to lift cookie out of pan; cool on a wire rack. Cool pan; line with clean foil. Repeat with the remaining dough.

3. Place ice cream in an extra-large bowl; stir until softened and spreadable. Add lemon curd and the 1 Tbsp. lemon zest; fold gently to swirl. Peel foil from cookies. Line the cooled baking pan with plastic wrap, extending wrap over edges of pan. Place one cookie in pan. Spread with ice cream mixture; top with the remaining cookie. Cover and freeze 4 hours or until firm. Use plastic wrap to lift uncut sandwiches out of pan. Cut into sandwiches. If desired, sprinkle sides with crushed candies.

NUMBER OF SERVINGS 40

PER SANDWICH *173 cal., 7 g fat (4 g sat. fat), 37 mg chol., 109 mg sodium, 27 g carb., 2 g fiber, 20 g sugars, 2 g pro.*

Wrap sandwiches individually with plastic wrap then place in an airtight container. Freeze up to 1 month.

FROZEN NEAPOLITANS

PREP 25 minutes **FREEZE** 5 hours **STAND** 10 minutes

4 cups chocolate-flavor crisp rice cereal

1¼ cups chopped toasted almonds

2 Tbsp. butter

2 cups tiny marshmallows

1 pt. chocolate ice cream

1 pt. vanilla ice cream

1 pt. strawberry ice cream

½ cup miniature semisweet chocolate pieces or ⅓ cup chocolate-flavor syrup or strawberry-flavor ice cream topping (optional)

1. Line a 13×9-inch baking pan with foil, extending foil over edges of pan. Butter foil. In a bowl combine cereal and ¾ cup of the almonds.

2. In a large saucepan melt butter over low heat. Add marshmallows; heat and stir until melted. Remove from heat. Add cereal mixture; stir gently to coat. Using a buttered rubber scraper or waxed paper, press mixture firmly into the prepared pan. Freeze 10 minutes.

3. Let each ice cream stand at room temperature 5 minutes to soften before spreading. Spread chocolate ice cream evenly over cereal layer. Freeze about 30 minutes or until firm. Spread vanilla ice cream over chocolate ice cream; freeze about 30 minutes or until firm. Spread strawberry ice cream over vanilla ice cream. Sprinkle with remaining ½ cup almonds. If desired, sprinkle with chocolate pieces or drizzle with chocolate syrup. Cover and freeze 4 hours or until firm.

4. Use foil to lift to Neapolitans out of pan. Cut into squares. Let stand 10 minutes before serving.

NUMBER OF SERVINGS 48

PER SQUARE *71 cal., 3 g fat (2 g sat. fat), 7 mg chol., 36 mg sodium, 9 g carb., 1 g fiber, 6 g sugars, 1 g pro.*

Place frozen squares in a single layer in an airtight container. Store in the freezer up to 1 month.

MAKE-IT-MINE NO-CHURN ICE CREAM

PREP 20 minutes **FREEZE** 8 hours

You don't need an ice cream maker to churn out a big batch of homemade ice cream. Use this stir-together recipe and "the pan" to make this rich-and-creamy treat. Experiment with a variety of stir-ins and ribbons, then write down your favorites.

BASE RECIPE

- 2 14-oz. cans sweetened condensed milk
- ¾ cup unsweetened cocoa powder (optional)
- 1 qt. heavy cream
- 1 Tbsp. vanilla
- 2 cups coarsely chopped Stir-In*
- 1 cup Ribbon

1. In an extra-large bowl stir together sweetened condensed milk and cocoa powder (if using). In another bowl beat cream and vanilla with a mixer on medium-high until soft peaks form (tips curl). Fold whipped cream into milk mixture. Fold in Stir-In. Spread half the cream mixture in a 3-qt. rectangular baking dish. Drizzle Ribbon over top. Spread remaining cream mixture over Ribbon layer.

2. Cover and freeze 8 hours or until firm.

NUMBER OF SERVINGS 24

PICK A STIR-IN

✳ **Chopped cookies** Peanut butter sandwich cookies with peanut butter filling, chocolate sandwich cookies with white filling, ginger snaps, vanilla wafers, shortbread cookies

✳ **Chopped candies** Chocolate-covered peanut butter cups, malted milk balls, chocolate-covered peanuts, peanut brittle, chocolate-covered toffee bars, candy-coated milk chocolate pieces, chocolate-coated caramel-topped nougat bars with peanuts, chocolate-covered crisp peanut butter candy

✳ **Chopped fruit** Bananas, peaches, strawberries, pitted sweet cherries, raspberries (do not chop)

*TIP If desired, combine different Stir-Ins to equal 2 cups, such as bananas and vanilla wafers, raspberries and shortbread cookies, or peaches and peanut brittle.

PICK A RIBBON

✳ Caramel or salted caramel ice cream topping

✳ Fudge ice cream topping

✳ Fruit preserves (strawberry, apricot, raspberry)

✳ Lemon, lime, or raspberry curd

✳ Marshmallow creme

OUR FAVORITES

(pictured top to bottom, opposite)

✳ Ribbon of strawberry preserves and lemon curd

✳ Chocolate-coated caramel-topped nougat bars with peanuts with marshmallow creme ribbon

✳ Chocolate sandwich cookies with white filling and fresh raspberries

✳ Plain with no Stir-In or Ribbon

BERRY-MELON SORBET

PREP 20 minutes **FREEZE** 6 hours

1 lime

1½ cups sugar

1½ cups water

1½ cups frozen raspberries

3 cups chopped seedless or seeds removed watermelon

1. Remove 1 Tbsp. zest and squeeze 3 Tbsp. juice from lime.

2. In a large saucepan combine sugar and the water. Bring to simmering over medium heat, stirring to dissolve sugar. Remove from heat. Add raspberries and lime juice. Stir to thaw raspberries.

3. Place raspberry mixture and watermelon in a food processor or blender. Cover and process until smooth. Press puree through a fine-mesh sieve; discard raspberry seeds. Stir in lime zest.

4. Transfer mixture to a 3-qt. rectangular baking dish. Cover; freeze 4 to 24 hours or until firm. Transfer to a chilled bowl, breaking up if necessary. Beat with a mixer on low to medium until smooth and lightened in color. Return to dish. Cover and freeze 2 to 4 hours or until firm.

NUMBER OF SERVINGS 14

PER ½ CUP *138 cal., 0 g fat, 0 mg chol., 2 mg sodium, 35 g carb., 2 g fiber, 33 g sugars, 1 g pro.*

Cover dish with plastic wrap then heavy foil. Freeze up to 1 month.

GREEN APPLE-CHARDONNAY GRANITA

PREP 20 minutes **FREEZE** 3 hours

This granita makes a refreshing adult dessert. Spoon into wine glasses and garnish with thinly sliced apple or halved fresh strawberries.

1 cup Chardonnay or other dry white wine

⅓ cup superfine sugar

1⅓ cups chopped Granny Smith apples

1½ cups apple juice

2 Tbsp. fresh lemon juice

1. In a bowl stir together wine and sugar until sugar is completely dissolved.

2. In a food processor or blender combine apples, ½ cup of the apple juice, and the lemon juice. Cover and process until smooth. Press mixture through a fine-mesh sieve, reserving apple liquid. Discard pulp. Add enough remaining apple juice to strained apple liquid to equal 2½ cups. Stir in wine mixture.

3. Transfer granita mixture to a 3-qt. rectangular baking dish. Freeze 1½ hours or until slushy. Stir with a fork; freeze 1½ to 2 hours more or until set. Using a fork, scrape granita into flakes.

NUMBER OF SERVINGS 8

PER ½ CUP *109 cal., 0 g fat, 0 mg chol., 4 mg sodium, 22 g carb., 2 g fiber, 19 g sugars, 0 pro.*

Prepare as directed, except do not scrape into flakes with a fork. Cover with plastic wrap then heavy foil. Freeze up to 1 month. Scrape into flakes as directed.

BLUEBERRY GRANITA FLOATS

PREP 30 minutes **FREEZE** 3 hours 15 minutes

1 lemon

1 cup water

¾ cup sugar

6 cups fresh blueberries

1 bottle sparkling rosé, chilled

1 pint coconut gelato

Honey

Fresh basil leaves

1. Remove 2 tsp. zest and squeeze 2 Tbsp. juice from lemon. In a medium saucepan combine lemon zest, the water, and sugar. Bring just to boiling over medium heat, stirring to dissolve sugar. Remove from heat; transfer to a large bowl. Freeze syrup 15 minutes.

2. Meanwhile, in a food processor combine 4 cups of the blueberries and the lemon juice. Process until nearly smooth. Strain blueberry puree through a fine-mesh sieve; discard pulp. Stir puree and ½ cup of the rosé into syrup (chill remaining rosé until needed). Pour mixture into a 3-qt. rectangular baking dish. Cover and freeze 1 hour. Scrape sides with a fork. Cover and freeze 2 hours more or until firm, scraping down sides once.

3. For floats, scoop coconut gelato into six 10- to 12-oz. glasses. Top each with a squeeze of honey and some of the remaining blueberries. Add a few scoops of blueberry granita to each and pour rosé over each. Top each with basil, and, if desired, a blueberry.

NUMBER OF SERVINGS 6

PER SERVING *368 cal., 6 g fat (4 g sat. fat), 20 mg chol., 42 mg sodium, 58 g carb., 3 g fiber, 52 g sugars, 3 g pro.*

Prepare as directed through Step 2. Cover with plastic wrap then heavy foil. Freeze up to 1 month.

INDEX

INDEX

PRODUCT DIFFERENCES

Most of the ingredients called for in the recipes in this book are available in most countries. However, some are known by different names. Here are some common American ingredients and their possible counterparts:

- Sugar (white) is granulated, fine granulated, or caster sugar.
- Powdered sugar is icing sugar.
- All-purpose flour is enriched bleached or unbleached white household flour. When self-rising flour is used in place of all-purpose flour in a recipe that calls for leavening, omit the leavening agent (baking soda or baking powder) and salt.
- Light-color corn syrup is golden syrup.
- Cornstarch is cornflour.
- Baking soda is bicarbonate of soda.
- Vanilla or vanilla extract is vanilla essence.
- Green, red, or yellow sweet peppers are capsicums or bell peppers.
- Golden raisins are sultanas.

VOLUME AND WEIGHT

The United States traditionally uses cup measures for liquid and solid ingredients. The chart (above right) shows the approximate imperial and metric equivalents. If you are accustomed to weighing solid ingredients, the following approximate equivalents will be helpful.

- 1 cup butter, caster sugar, or rice = 8 ounces = ½ pound = 250 grams
- 1 cup flour = 4 ounces = ¼ pound = 125 grams
- 1 cup icing sugar = 5 ounces = 150 grams
- Canadian and U.S. volume for a cup measure is 8 fluid ounces (237 ml), but the standard metric equivalent is 250 ml.
- 1 British imperial cup is 10 fluid ounces.
- In Australia, 1 tablespoon equals 20 ml, and there are 4 teaspoons in the Australian tablespoon.
- Spoon measures are used for small amounts of ingredients. Although the size of the tablespoon varies slightly in different countries, for practical purposes and for recipes in this book, a straight substitution is all that's necessary. Measurements made using cups or spoons always should be level unless stated otherwise.

COMMON WEIGHT RANGE REPLACEMENTS

Imperial / U.S.	Metric
½ ounce	15 g
1 ounce	25 g or 30 g
4 ounces (¼ pound)	115 g or 125 g
8 ounces (½ pound)	225 g or 250 g
16 ounces (1 pound)	450 g or 500 g
1¼ pounds	625 g
1½ pounds	750 g
2 pounds or 2¼ pounds	1,000 g or 1 Kg

OVEN TEMPERATURE EQUIVALENTS

Fahrenheit Setting	Celsius Setting	Gas Setting
300°F	150°C	Gas Mark 2 (very low)
325°F	160°C	Gas Mark 3 (low)
350°F	180°C	Gas Mark 4 (moderate)
375°F	190°C	Gas Mark 5 (moderate)
400°F	200°C	Gas Mark 6 (hot)
425°F	220°C	Gas Mark 7 (hot)
450°F	230°C	Gas Mark 8 (very hot)
475°F	240°C	Gas Mark 9 (very hot)
500°F	260°C	Gas Mark 10 (extremely hot)
Broil	Broil	Grill

*Electric and gas ovens may be calibrated using celsius. However, for an electric oven, increase celsius setting 10 to 20 degrees when cooking above 160°C. For convection or forced air ovens (gas or electric), lower the temperature setting 25°F/10°C when cooking at all heat levels.

BAKING PAN SIZES

Imperial / U.S.	Metric
9×1½-inch round cake pan	22- or 23×4-cm (1.5 L)
9×1½-inch pie plate	22- or 23×4-cm (1 L)
8×8×2-inch square cake pan	20×5-cm (2 L)
9×9×2-inch square cake pan	22- or 23×4.5-cm (2.5 L)
11×7×1½-inch baking pan	28×17×4-cm (2 L)
2-quart rectangular baking pan	30×19×4.5-cm (3 L)
13×9×2-inch baking pan	34×22×4.5-cm (3.5 L)
15×10×1-inch jelly roll pan	40×25×2-cm
9×5×3-inch loaf pan	23×13×8-cm (2 L)
2-quart casserole	2 L

U.S. / STANDARD METRIC EQUIVALENTS

⅛ teaspoon = 0.5 ml	
¼ teaspoon = 1 ml	
½ teaspoon = 2 ml	
1 teaspoon = 5 ml	
1 tablespoon = 15 ml	
2 tablespoons = 25 ml	
¼ cup = 2 fluid ounces = 50 ml	
⅓ cup = 3 fluid ounces = 75 ml	
½ cup = 4 fluid ounces = 125 ml	
⅔ cup = 5 fluid ounces = 150 ml	
¾ cup = 6 fluid ounces = 175 ml	
1 cup = 8 fluid ounces = 250 ml	
2 cups = 1 pint = 500 ml	
1 quart = 1 litre	